Railway Track Diagrams

Book 5:
Southern and TfL

Edited by Gerald Jacobs

TRACKmaps

1st Edition 1994
2nd Edition 2002
3rd Edition 2008

ISBN 978-0-9549866-4-3

Published by TRACKmaps Little Court, Upper South Wraxall, Bradford on Avon BA15 2SE
(Tel: 0845 300 1370 Fax: 0845 300 1375)
Web: www.trackmaps.co.uk Email: sales@trackmaps.co.uk

Edited by Gerald Jacobs

Original Cartography by John Yonge

Digital Conversion & Design by ESR Cartography Ltd
Woodley, Reading RG5 3LE

Printed by Brightsea Press,
Exeter EX5 2UL

Railway Track Diagrams
Book 5: Southern & TfL
Editor: Gerald Jacobs

Preface to the Third Edition

Quail Track Diagrams have been published since 1988 and provide a reference to Enthusiasts and Industry alike. They contain information which may exist elsewhere and in other forms but are unique in making it all available in one easily portable volume.

Originally published by the Quail Map Co, edited by Gerald Jacobs with cartography by John Yonge, the series covers the entire UK mainland network on the basis of the original British Rail regions and includes private railways and Transport for London.

The information included is a combination of historical sources collected by Gerald Jacobs during his 40 years with British Railways, added to subsequently, kept up to date with reference to Network Rail and its predecessors and supplemented by other data, by the kind assistance of other persons and by field observation. The Railway Track Diagrams have become standard reference works for a wide range of users from train staff and infrastructure managers to railway enthusiast and modellers.

In 2004, Trackmaps took over the publication of these volumes and embarked on the digital conversion of the information at same time as incorporating updates. This Book was previously updated in 2002 and represents a tremendous amount of work in catching up the intervening years. With the production of this title, the first full cycle is complete and all 5 books now follow the same format. The update cycle now begins again.

TRACKmaps, November 2008

Introduction

The Track Diagrams in this book cover the lines forming the Kent, Sussex and Wessex Routes of Network Rail, together with a small part of adjoining Routes and a number of private railways and industrial layouts. They are, in general, up to date as at November 2008.

However, records are wonderful things. They can both inform and confuse. Nowhere is this more certain than on the UK Railway Network. Built up, as it has been, over more than 180 years, managed as individual companies, as a nationalised industry and now as individual train operating companies with a single infrastructure owner, it has grown, stagnated, declined and grown again more than once within that time. Many persons have produced records and maps at different times for different parts, both within the industry and outside. Many record systems compete for information or act in a complementary manner to each other. Track Diagrams attempt to collate these diverse sources into one publication but, even so, space precludes the inclusion of much detail including, for example, signals.

Track Diagrams also try to put down a standard where discrepancies occur; mileages are typical. Mileages often vary slightly between different official records but, in general, those given in Sectional Appendix have been used. Station mileages are usually taken from the mid-point of the platforms or, in the case of a terminus, the buffer stops. The Railway is continually changing and, because of its diverse nature and varied history, discrepancies often arise between seeming accurate sources. In such circumstances, the Editor's judgment is applied.

Acknowledgments

A large number of people have contributed to the information in this publication, some in a significant way providing layouts, site checking or proofing details and some in a small way giving personal observations, answering individual questions or giving access to engineering drawings and construction diagrams. The assistance of all is gratefully acknowledged, especially persons at Network Rail. Other contributing individuals include persons at EWS Railways, together with Iain Scotchman, Michael Oakley and Simon Lowe. Acknowledgements are also due to the Branch Line Society, the Railway Correspondence & Travel Society and many other correspondents, railway societies and representatives of the private and preserved systems featured, including Peter Scott (see his website http://web.ukonline.co.uk/pe.scott)

The digital production of this book could not have proceeded without the efforts of the team at ESR Cartography Ltd but special thanks must also be given to two people; firstly, to John Yonge, the originator of the track diagram artwork, whose cartography and advice provided a sound basis of the maps in the book; and, secondly, to Elvina Jacobs for her forbearance and continuous support given throughout the Editor's long and arduous task.

Gerald Jacobs

KEY

————	Running Line
————	Siding
————	Electrified overhead
————	Electrified 3rd rail
————	Electrified 3rd rail (Underail contact, DLR)
————	Electrified 4th rail (LU)
————	Electrified, overhead & Conductor rail

A broken line indicates 'in situ' but out of use, proposed or under construction.

——●——	Line obstructed
——○——	Line out of use
⋮	Change of Signalling mandate
W ᵾ WX	Network Rail Territory / Route Boundary
London | Three Bridge | Bridges (L) | (T)	Signal Box / Signalling Centre area limits (Within an area, plates on automatic signals may reflect actual line description)
—)---(—	Tunnel
≈	Bridge under Rail or Viaduct
—┤—	Selected Motorway / Trunk Road bridges over rail
—┼—	Network Rail operated level crossing
┆	User-worked crossing with Telephone
←——→	Track signalled in both directions (a double arrow indicates normal direction of travel) (On single lines 'DN' indicates down direction)
⧖	Private siding boundary, often marked by a gate
—————┤	Buffer Stop
—————⌐	Sand Drag
—— A □	Friction Arrester
—⊘—	Turntable
....	Gantry Rails (Freightliner Terminal)
wwwwwww	Wall / Bank
═══▲═══	Hot Axle Box Detector (HABD), Wheel Impact Load Detector (WILD), Wheelchex Device or Vehicle Health Monitoring Equipment (VHME)

[SMS]	ELR-Engineer's Line Reference (Prefix and suffix numbers indicate sub-divisions and their boundaries)
[SO 130]	Line of Route Code Double entries occur on short linking sections
| 93	Whole mileposts, shown on the appropriate side of the line
| 32	Whole kilometre posts
81.3⌐	End of mileage run
113.76 / 105.70 COM	Lineside mileage change
3	Platform with number (May be supplemented by sub-divisions. e.g. (a), (b), (c), 'N' or North etc)
⑦	Indicates number of carriages per platform (approx 20m lengths, the actual number may be less to accomodate operational restrictions)
⬚	Provisional proposed platform
▭	Former Royal Mail platform
▭	Platform out of use
⊔	Other feature (labelled)
▨	Loading bank
Three Bridges (T) ⊠	Signal Box or Signalling Centre, with code (underlined text relates to SB or SC)
▣	Signal Room on CTRL only
☑	Control Panel
⧖	Gate Box
⊡ ⊙	Ground Frame/Ground Switch Panel or Shunting Frame. ⓢ Indicates 'Shut in' facility
✳	Radio electronic token block / Token exchange point
○	Water tower
∧ ∨ ⇈	Significant changes in gradient; summit trough and others
(Lullingstone) ●	Indicates a former Jn, Station or Signal Box
86.34 (Not italic if Station mileage)	Distance in miles and chains from specified zero 1 mile = 1760 yards / 1.6km 80 chains = 1 mile 1 chain = 22 yards / 20.11m
57.60 km	Distance in kilometres

Guide references are given to pre-nationalisation, pre-grouping and sometimes pioneer railways e.g. S : LSW (London & Southampton)

London Underground Signalling

LU signalling is controlled at some places by local Signal Cabins, or for a long part or the whole of some lines by Signal Control Centres. Because of different cables, LU has Interlocking Machines operated by air motors (or comparable equipment) in unmanned rooms near points, except where a local cabin has an interlocking lever frame. IMR's (and equivalent rooms) are included in these maps, but purely Relay Rooms (and their equivalents) are not. IMR's bear the name of the adjacent station unless otherwise noted: (e) indicates location at the end of the platform, (m) in the middle of the platform.

Symbol	Description	Symbol	Description
▢ (MAA)	Local Cabin or Control Centre with code(s) controlled	(NP)	Interlocking within manned cabin, with code(s), controlled
(MU)	Unmanned Interlocking Machine (or comparable equipment) Room, with code	⊡	Ground Frame
(NP)	Interlocking inside former cabin, with code	| BR | BS	Code area boundaries (where not separated by a long stretch of plain track(s))
		(TR) | (CAW)	Signal Area / Station Identity

Publisher's Note

Every effort has been made by the editor to ensure the accuracy of the information in the book is as correct as possible at the time of going to press. Notwithstanding, the Publisher welcomes corrections, updates or suggestions for application to future editions.

GENERAL ABBREVIATIONS

AA	Acid Application	FA	Flushing Apron	PW	Permanent Way
ABP	Associated British Ports	FP	Fuelling Point or Footpath	Qy	Query concerning distances etc, unresolved
AC	Alternating Current	ft	Feet	REC	Reception
ARR	Arrival	GB	Gate Box	RETB	Radio Electronic Token Block
ASC	Area Signalling Centre i/c IECC, Power Box	GC	Gantry Crane	REV	Reversing or Reversible line
bdy	boundary	GDS	Goods	RR	Run-Round
BCH	Branch	GF	Ground Frame	S	South
BR	British Rail	GL	Goods Loop	S & T	Signal & Telegraph
CCTV	Closed Circuit Television	GS	Goods Shed	SB	Signal Box or Southbound
CET	Controlled Emission Toilet Discharge	GSP	Ground Switch Panel	SC	Signalling Centre
CL	Crossing Loop on Single Line	H	Headshunt	SCC	Signalling Control Centre
COM	Change of Lineside Mileage	HH	Hopper House	Sdg(s)	Siding(s)
CR	Cripple Siding	HST	High Speed Train	SD	Sand Drag
CW	Carriage Washer	IECC	Integrated Electronic Control Centre	SF	Shunting Frame
C&W	Carriage & Wagon	Jn	Junction	SIMBIDS	Simplified Bi-Directional Signalling
D	Connections Disconnected	Jt	Joint	SN	Shunt Neck
DA	Down Avoiding	km	kilometres	SP	Switch Panel/Servicing Platform
DC	Direct Current	L	Wheel Lathe	SS	Shunt Spur
DE	Down Electric	LC	Level Crossing (manned, automatic or open)	TA	Tamper Siding
DED	Diesel Electric Depot	LHS	Locomotive Holding Siding	TB	Turnback Siding
DEP	Departure	LP	Loop	TEP	Token Exchange Point
DF	Down Fast	LPG	Liquified petroleum gas	TL	Traffic Lights
DG	Down Goods	LS	Locomotive Shed	TMD	Traction Maintenance Depot
DGL	Down Goods Loop	LW	Locomotive Washer	T&RSMD	Traction & Rolling Stock Maintenance Depot
DL	Down Loop	M	Middle	TS	Through Siding
DM	Down Main	M ch	Miles and Chains	U&D	Up & Down
DMD	Diesel Maintenance Depot	M&EE	Mechanical & Electrical Engineer	UA	Up Avoiding
DMUD	Diesel Multiple Unit Depot	MGR	'Merry-go-round'	UE	Up Electric
DN	Down	MN	Main	UF	Up Fast
DPL	Down Passenger Loop	MOD	Ministry of Defence	UFN	Until Further Notice
DR	Down Relief	MU	Maintenance Unit	UG	Up Goods
DRS	Down Refuge Sidings	N	North	UGL	Up Goods Loop
DS	Down Slow	n	not electrified	UH	Unloading Hopper
DSB	Down Suburban	NB	Northbound	UL	Up Loop
DT	Down Through	NIRU	Not in regular use	UM	Up Main
E	East	NR	Network Rail	UPL	Up Passenger Loop
EB	Eastbound	NT	No Telephone provided	UR	Up Relief
EGF	Emergency Ground Frame	OHC	Overhead Crane	URS	Up Refuge Siding
EMD	Electric Maintenance Depot	OHLE	Overhead Line Equipment	US	Up Slow
EMUD	Electric Multiple Unit Depot	OOU	Out of Use	USB	Up Suburban
Engrs	Engineers' Sidings	OTM	On-track Maintenance	UT	Up Through
eol	End of Line	P	Points padlocked	V or Vdct	Viaduct
ESP	Emergency Signalling Panel	PAD	Prefabricated Assembly Depot	W	West
EWS	English Welsh & Scottish Railway Ltd	PL	Passenger Loop	WB	Westbound or Weighbridge
F	Fence across track	PS	Private Siding	WD	War Department or Wheelchex Device
		PSB	Power Signal Box	yds	yards

SUPPLEMENTARY ABBREVIATIONS FOR THIS BOOK

CTRL	Channel Tunnel Rail Link	LU	London Underground
ER	Eastern Region	MSW	former Midland and South Western Jn Railway
ET	Eurotunnel	N&SWJn	former North and South Western Jn Railway
GC	former Great Central Railway	RFF	Réseau Ferré de France
GE	former Great Eastern Railway	S	former Southern Railway
GN	former Great Northern Railway	SE	former South Eastern Railway
GW	former Great Western Railway	SNCF	Société Nationale des Chemins de Fer Français (French National Railways)
LBSC	former London, Brighton and South Coast Railway		
LCD	former London, Chatham and Dover Railway	SO	Southern Region
LGV	Ligne à Grande Vitesse (High Speed Line)	TfL	Transport for London
LMS	former London Midland and Scottish Railway	TGV	Train à Grande Vitesse (High Speed Train)
LNE	former London and North Eastern Railway	WL	former West London Joint Railway
LNW	former London and North Western Railway	WLE	former West London Extension Joint Railway
LPTB	former London Passenger Transport Board		
LSW	former London and South Western Railway		

LEVEL CROSSING ABBREVIATIONS

STANDARD	Supplementary	Description	STANDARD	Supplementary	Description
(ABCL) *		Automatic Barrier Crossing, road warning lights and barriers monitored by Traincrew		(MWLF)	Miniature Warning Lights at user-worked Footpath
				(MWLG)	Miniature Warning Lights with Gates
(AHBC) *		Automatic Half-Barrier Crossing		(MWLO)	Miniature Warning Lights at Open crossing
(AOCL) *		Automatic Open Crossing, road warning lights and barriers monitored by Traincrew	(OC)	(O) (OPEN)	Open Crossing (non-automatic), without barriers, gates or road traffic signals
	(AOCR)	Automatic Open Crossing, Remotely monitored	(RC)		Remotely Controlled manned Level Crossing (gates) operated locally by Signaller or Crossing Keeper
	(BW)	Bridle Way			
(CCTV)		Manned Level Crossing (full barriers) with Closed Circuit Television	(R/G)		Miniature Red and Green warning lights i/c Miniature Stop Lights operated by approaching trains
	(FP (B)(G)(K)(W))	Footpath crossing (only shown if telephone provided) (B) Barriers, (G) Gates, (K) Kissing Gate, (W) Wickets	(TMO)		Traincrew Operated crossing
				(TMOB)	Traincrew Operated Barrier
(MCB)	(MB)	Manned Level Crossing (barriers) operated locally by Signaller or Crossing Keeper		(TMOG)	Traincrew Operated Gates
			(UWC)	(UWCP)	User-Worked Crossing of occupation, accommodation or bridleway status
	(MCBR)	Manned Level Crossing with Barriers, Remotely controlled		(UWB)	User-Worked Barriers
(MG)	(MCG)	Manned Level Crossing (gates) operated locally by Signaller or Crossing Keeper		(UWCM)	User-Worked Crossing with miniature Red and Green warning lights
	(MGH)	Manned Gates, Hand worked		(UWG)	User-Worked Gates
	(MGW)	Manned Gates with Wickets		(UWK)	User-Worked with Kissing Gates
	(MSL (B)(F)(G))	Miniature Stop Light with (B) Barriers, (F) Footpath, (G) Gates		(UWS)	User-Worked Stile
				(UWW)	User-Worked Wickets
	(MWL)	Miniature Warning Lights		(WL)	Barrow or Foot Crossing with White Light indicators
	(MWLB)	Miniature Warning Lights with Barriers			

* (-X) shown after these abbreviations e.g. (AHBC-X) indicates that the crossing works automatically for movements in the wrong direction.

In some cases, the code of the controlling signal box may be shown e.g. (AHBC-X) (KS)

If no abbreviation is shown, the level crossing is either operated locally by a Signaller or Crossing Keeper or privately but equipped with a telephone.

Controlled by Marylebone SC (ME)

MCJ 1
NAJ 1
NJN part

NAJ 1 [MD 701] LNE : GC

3 : 19A : to S. Ruislip & Birmingham

3 : 18D : 5 : 42B : to Harrow-on-the-Hill etc

4 : 1L to Bedford

Neasden Freight Terminal

a = NEASDEN CURVE [MD 715] NJN LNE : GC [EA 1360]

§ = 201.09 [MD 701] MCJ 1 LNE : GC

41A : & 4 : 8A to Watford Jn + Bakerloo Line to Harrow & Wealdstone

✳ = LU km distances from zero at Ongar

NEASDEN (200.76)

Dudding Hill Jn (DH) 6.03

HARLESDEN 6.08 (55.41km)

Neasden Jn (NJ) 7.03 / 6.56

[MD 155] KGC LMS : LNW

Willesden H.L. Jn (HL) Controls
BOK 2/3/4
KGC part
KGW part
WMB part

For full details of Willesden area see 4 : 1 & 8

4 : 8A : to Wembley Central & North

4 : 8A : to Wembley Yard & Nth

LLG [MD 101]

✱ LLG [MD 101] LMS : LNW
Miles from Willesden No. 1 WLL Jn

CAW LMS : Mid

e = LNW(S)(WM) [MD 165] ANG (AW) [EA 1360]

f = |8.77| 7.03 (St Pancras)

g = 0.66 Acton Wells Jn |7.07| Falcon Jn (0.58 Willesden HL Jn)

✱ (Acton Wells Jn) Controls
ACW   BOK 4&5
AWL   CAW

ACW [EA 1360]
WAW LMS : N & SW Jn
BOK 4 [EA 1310] Old Oak Sdgs

Acton Canal Wharf (ACW) 8.41
Acton Canal Wharf Jn 8.45

3 : 1B : To West Ruislip ANL GW
37B : LUL Central Line to West Ruislip & Ealing Broadway

43B,C : District Line to Ealing B'way, Piccadilly Line to Rayners Lane

Acton Rail Terminal

Details of London Underground Lines on : 37B, 43B

COM (Goods Lines) [GW 130] AWL [EA 1310]

Acton Wells Jn 0.64

(Poplar Jn) Acton East Jn 0.08

3 : 2A : to Reading, West of England & South Wales

ACTON MAIN LINE 4.21

BOK 5 LMS : N & SW Jn

EALING BROADWAY 5.56
MLN 1 GW
Miles from Paddington

43B : District & Piccadilly Lines to Acton Town

Acton Wells Jn (AW)
Bollo Lane (BL)
Toilet Discharge Sdgs

W routes
ANL [GW 110]
AWL [GW 130] **Controlled by 'Slough New' ASC (SN)**
MLN [GW 103]

To Acton Town

Churchfield Rd (CCTV) 1.70
ACTON CENTRAL 1.73 (AC/DC changeover)

Bollo Lane (Kew Line) (CCTV) 2.63

SOUTH ACTON 2.48
2.52 South Acton Jn

6 BOK 5 [EA 1330] LMS: N & SW Jn
Kew East Jn (KE)

Old Kew Jn (3.73)

SAR 1 [EA 1310]
Bollo Lane (BL) (MCB) 2.63 (Richmond Line)

44A : LU District & Piccadilly Line
9.53 (51.70km) Acton Lane Jn (AN)

BRENTFORD 10.52

BRB GW bridge 11.03

Miles from Waterloo via Barnes

KEW BRIDGE 9.53
New Kew Jn

COM 9.76 Gunnersbury Jn

GUNNERSBURY 10.05 (52.33km)
Miles from Waterloo via Kensington and Turnham Green

SYON LANE 11.34

10.68 Grand Jn Canal

HOU S : LSW
NKE S : LSW
Kew Bridge (River Thames)

Grove Park (CCTV-F)
(F) Feltham 8.75 (W) Wimbledon

ISLEWORTH 12.10

Wood Lane (CCTV-F) 11.69

KEW GARDENS 11.10 (54.05km)

CHISWICK 8.47

Miles from Waterloo via Putney

HOUNSLOW SPUR ✱ HJW S : LSW [SW 210] [SW 230]

HOU S : LSW

HOUNSLOW 13.40

TWICKENHAM 11.22

Controlled by Feltham (F) ASC
[SW 210] RDG 1 S : LSW

Platforms (SW) 1,2 (NL) 3,4,5 (LU) 6,7
RICHMOND (GB) 12.22 / 12.39 (56.16km)

SAR 2 S : LSW

Hounslow Jn 14.09
Whitton Jn

Pope's Grove Viaduct and arches, not continuous

Old Deer Park Viaduct

NORTH SHEEN 9.03

MORTLAKE 8.21

Feltham Jn 12.43
WHITTON
RDG 1 S : LSW

Twickenham Jn 11.69

ST. MARGARETS 10.66

Richmond Bridge (R. Thames)
RICHMOND 9.57

White Hart Lane (CCTV-W) 7.52

25A : to Feltham & Staines

STRAWBERRY HILL 12.22
[SW 245] TSJ S : LSW
21B : to Shepperton

Miles from Waterloo via Putney

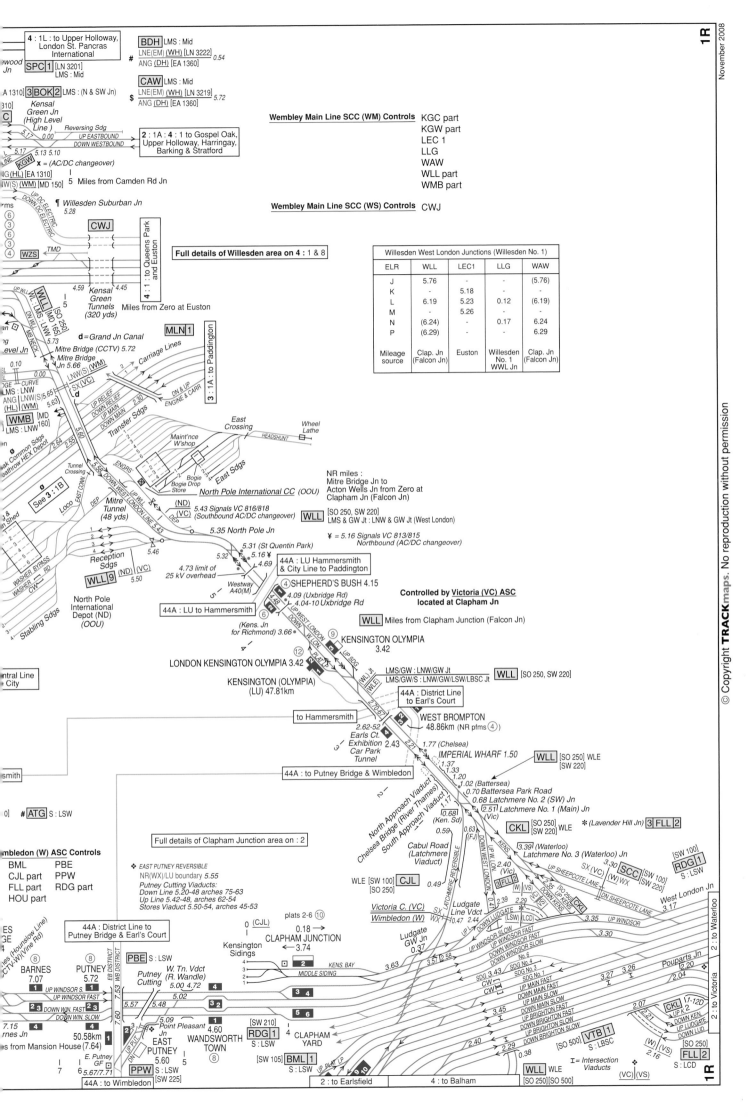

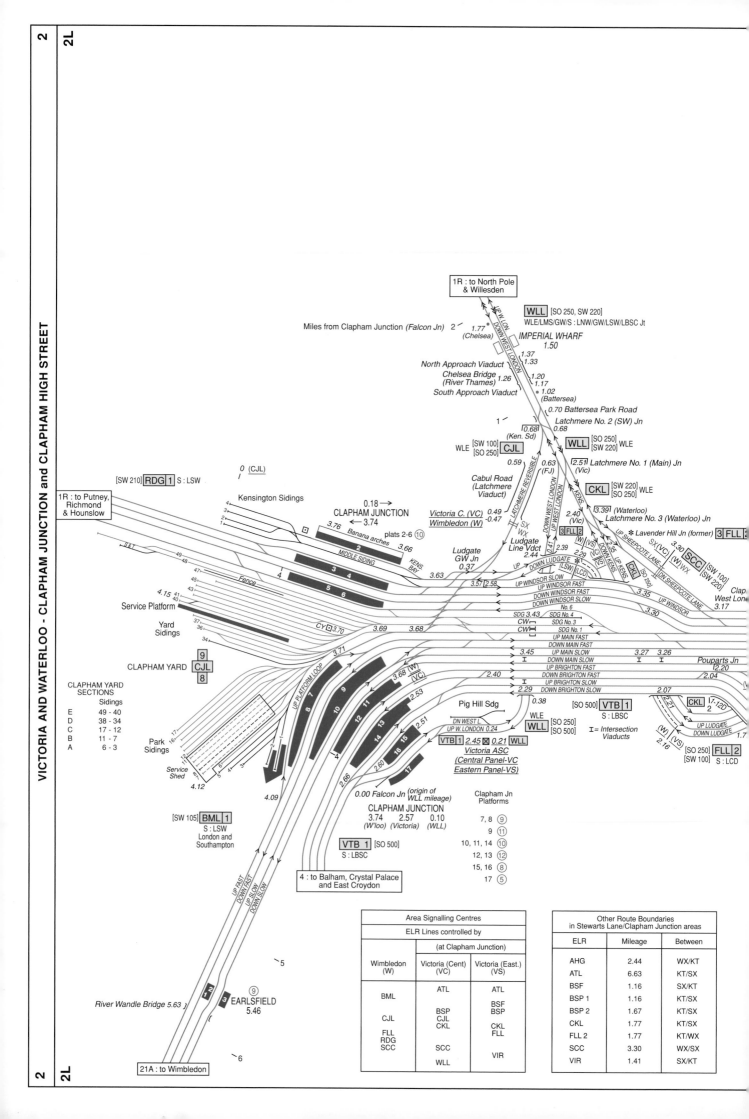

LONDON VICTORIA
0.00

LONDON WATERLOO 0.05

(Mileage origin 0.00 at junction with former SE Rly)

Platforms 21-24 OOU

0.06

NB: Slight chainage variations occur with buffer stop locations

0.00 (4-7)
0.01 (2 & 3)
0.03 (8)
0.05

Eccleston Bridge 0.10

0.15 0.12 0.10

Platforms
1 (13)
2 (14/17)
3 (8)
4-6 (10)
7 (13)
8 (9)
-19 (12)

0.17 0.17 0.18

0.20

Elizabeth Bridge 0.21

0.21

[SO 500] VTB 1
S : LBSC

Outbound Gantry 0.28

[SO 110] VIR (VS)
S : LCD

Ebury Bridge 0.33
0.38

Up Carriage Sdgs
(Pugs Hole)
Inbound Gantry 0.35

Controlled by
Victoria (VC) ASC
located at Clapham Junction

Controlled by
Victoria (VS) ASC
located at Clapham Junction

0.56

Victoria (Grosvenor) Carriage Shed
0.51
'A'   'B' Section

Grosvenor Bridge (River Thames) 0.65

0.71 (arch 759)
Battersea Pier Sidings
Staff Halt 0.72

(0.71 (arch 759)
0.72

Battersea Pier Jn

0.78 (arch 742)

Battersea Pier Sdgs

[SO 110] BSF
S : LCD

a = Engine Viaduct
b = Battersea Dog's Home Viaduct
c = Havelock Terrace Viaduct
d = Pagden Street Viaduct
e = Gladstone Terrace Viaduct

1.01

(724)

(arch 723)

(arch 714)
(arch 713)

7.27 (Lon. Br.)

1.05

Battersea Park Jn

Platforms
1 (6)
2 (4)
3-5 (8)

BATTERSEA PARK
1.23
Viaduct (arches 50B-100)

[SO 500] VTB 2
S : LBSC

[SO 250]

7.35

1.13

1.18

1.23

BSP [SO 110]
1.26

$ = UMF to UMS crossover OOU

VAUXHALL
1.29

[SW 100] RDG 1
S : LSW

[SW 100] RDG 1
S : LSW

50B

QUEENSTOWN RD (Battersea)

2.54

ATL LBSC

VIR [SO 110]
(VC) (VS)

* Wheel Chex 2.44 UMF and UMS

BML 1

* = UMF to UMS crossover OOU

2.65

2.61

1.42

(BML)

2.61 Q'town Rd V.
Longhedge Jns (C,B,A)

2.52

S : LBSC

arches 692-695

2.49-13
Nine Elms flyover
2.08 Nine Elms Viaduct (arches 1-72)

2.31 (W)(VS) Down

Nine Elms Jn 1.78 WIN REV

UP WATERLOO CURVE
DN WATERLOO CURVE

(VS)(W) Up

UP WIN
DN W.F
UP W.S
DN W.S
UP M.F
DN M.F
UP M.S
DN M.S

7.12

2.50 UP M.F
2.42 2.38
1.31 (VIR)

AHG BR
Stewarts Lane Viaduct

[SW 100] BSP 1 [SO 250]

1.48 RUN ROUND

Stewarts Lane Jn 1/2
A691

1.45 (Vic.), 2.50 (Wat.) Linford Street Jn

[SW 100] BML 1 S : LSW

FLL Viaducts from Longhedge Jn (A) to Factory Jn

		Arches
h = Coal Sidings Viaduct (339)	0.16 - 0.19	84 - 82
k = Old Loco Sdgs Viaduct (340)	0.19 - 0.20	81 - 77
l = South London Line Viaduct (341)	0.22 - 0.25	76 - 70
m = Old Goods Sdgs Viaduct (342)	0.26 - 0.41	69 - 56

ATL Viaducts from Shepherds Lane Jn to Battersea Park Stn

		Arches
s = Voltaire Road Viaduct	6.15 - 6.17	641 - 644A
t = Portslade Road Viaduct	6.56 - 6.75	1 - 22
u = Carriage Shed Viaduct	6.75 - 7.00	23 - 43
w = Stewarts Lane Viaduct	7.00 - 7.06	44 - 49
x = Ingate Place Viaduct	7.06 - 7.12	50 - 58
y = Patcham Terrace Viaduct	7.13 - 7.18	59 - 73
z = Battersea Park Viaduct	7.22 - 7.26	74 - 80

VIR Viaducts from Clapham High St. Stn to Shepherds Lane Jn

		Arches
p = Voltaire Road Viaduct	2.29 - 2.32	644A - 641
q = Lendal Terrace Viaduct	2.32 - 2.37	640 - 631
r = Cottage Grove Viaduct	2.37 - 2.39	630 - 628A

STEWARTS LANE
Traction & Rolling Stock
Maintenance Depot (SL)

SLC

SLC 8

Carriage Servicing
and Inspection Shed

Longhedge Junctions

	BSP	FLL	CKL
A	1.58	0.09	-
B	1.63	-	1.63
C	-	1.67	1.67

Factory Junctions

ELR	ATL	BSF	FLL	VIR
A	6.58	1.75	-	1.68
B	6.67	1.67	-	(1.75)
C	6.67	1.67	0.41	-

c = Carriage & wagon shed
& Venice-Simplon Orient Express (VSOE) SLC 1

d = Electric loco. running shed
with wheel lathe at end of no. 3 road

WANDSWORTH ROAD
(LB)6.52 (1.75)(Vic)

Voltaire Road Jn

CLAPHAM HIGH STREET
(LB)6.21 (2.25)(Vic)

Miles from Victoria (E)
via Chatham Main Line

[SO 110] VIR S : LCD

Shepherds Lane Jn 2.67 (Vic.) Vdct

3A : to Brixton, Herne Hill, Elephant & Castle, Peckham Rye & Nunhead

3A : to Peckham Rye & London Bridge

DOWN CHATHAM MAIN
UP CHATHAM MAIN
DOWN ATLANTIC (2.62)
UP ATLANTIC

6.14-09
Lendal Terrace Viaduct

6.08-06
Cottage Grove Viaduct

5.68 (London Bridge)

5.50
Shepherds Lane Viaduct

[SO 645] ATL S : LCD

Miles from London Bridge *via Denmark Hill*

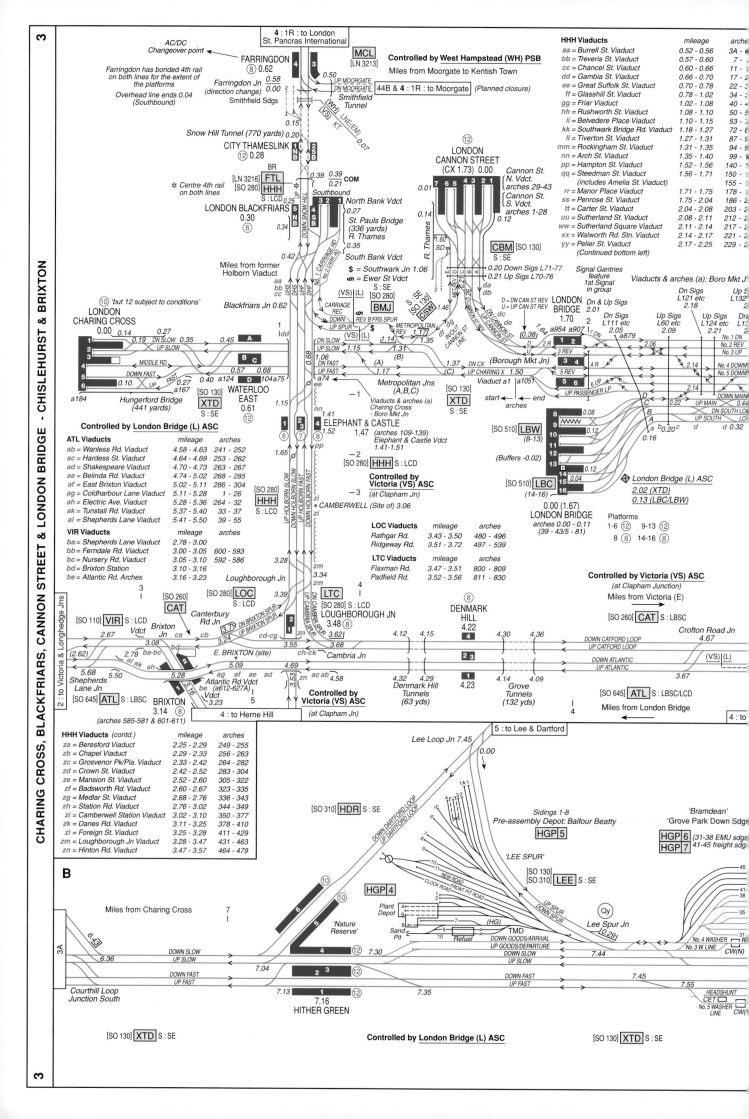

LBC & LBW Viaducts

	mileage	LBC arches	LBW arches
a = St. Thomas St. Viaduct	0.04 - 0.19	various	various
b = (Unamed)	0.19 - 0.20	1, 2	various
c = Brunswick Viaduct	0.20 - 0.23	3 - 6	859 - 856
d = Roper Lane Viaduct	0.23 - 0.30	7A - 17C	854 - 839
e = Bacons Viaduct	0.32 - 0.35	22 - 28C	833 - 826
f = Tanner Viaduct	0.35 - 0.38	30 - 33C	825 - 811
g = Maltby Viaduct	0.38 - 0.45	34A - 54C	809 - 788
h = Marquis of Wellington Viaduct	0.45 - 0.50	55A - 66B	785 - 775
i = Perseverance Viaduct	0.50 - 0.53	67C - 71B	773 - 763
k = Bevingtons Viaduct	0.53 - 0.67	72A - 105C	760A - 724
l = Enid St. Viaduct	0.67 - 0.69	106A - 110B	722 - 713
m = Dockley Rd. Viaduct	0.69 - 0.74	111A - 120	708 - 700
n = Lucey Rd. Viaduct	0.74 - 1.01	123 - 140	697 - 680
p = Clement's Viaduct	1.05 - 1.08	144 - 160B	676 - 661
q = Blue Anchor Viaduct	1.08 - 1.28	161C - 215C	654 - 596
r = Almond Rd. Arches	1.28 - 1.48	1A - 45	1.28 - 1.60
s = Rotherhithe Rd. Arches	1.49 - 1.59	46 - 54	592 - 500
t = Jarrow Rd. Arches	1.61 - 1.66	1 - 14	1.60 - 1.62
			500A - 500L

CBM Viaducts

	mileage	arches
da = Crown Wharf Viaduct	0.20 - 0.21	235 - 233
db = Park St. Viaducts North	0.21 - 0.27	232 - 205
dc = Winchester Viaduct	0.27 - 0.29	203 - 201
de = Borough Market Viaduct	0.29 - 0.33	

CSW Viaducts

	mileage	arches
df = Redcross Viaduct	1.37 - 1.41	185 - 190
dg = Park St. Viaducts South	1.41 - 1.46	192 - 199

NKL Viaducts

	mileage	arches
na = Childers St. Viaduct	4.24 - 4.26	328 - 321
nb = Etta St. Viaduct	4.26 - 4.34	295 - 282
nc = Dorking Rd. Viaduct	4.34 - 4.45	278 - 246
nd = Kerry Rd. Viaduct	4.45 - 4.57	243 - 208
ne = Edward Place Viaduct	4.57 - 4.60	206 - 200
nf = Payne St. Viaduct	4.60 - 4.66	197 - 179
ng = Ffinch St. Viaduct	4.66 - 4.76	177 - 130
nh = Mechanics Path Viaduct	4.76 - 5.08	128 - 97
ni = Browne House Viaduct	5.08 - 5.11	95 - 87
nj = Farrer House Viaduct	5.11 - 5.15	85 - 76
nk = Sun Wharf Viaduct	5.15 - 5.20	74 - 60
nl = Harts Wharf Viaduct	5.20 - 5.26	57 - 45
nm = Brewery Viaduct	5.26 - 5.28	42 - 35

Viaducts and arches east of London Bridge
ELR routes XTD, LBW, LBC

Routes XTD & LBW share the arches of the
former London & Greenwich Rly. to arch 593
From arch 593 (XTD 3.17, LBC & LBW 1m 28ch)
the LBC route separates
From arch 500 (XTD 3m 48ch, LBW 1m 60ch)
the LBW route separates
From arch 470 (XTD 3m 54ch) the New Cross
Spur separates

Controlled by **London Bridge (L) ASC**

Miles from Charing Cross

Viaducts & arches (a): Boro Mkt Jn - Greenwich

[SO 130] XTD S : SE

[SO 290] NKL
S : SE (London & Greenwich)

46B : to Dalston

CAT Viaducts

	mileage	arches
ca = Station Rd. Viaduct	3.08 - 3.16	580 - 571
cb = Popes Viaduct	3.16 - 3.24	570 - 555
cd = Canterbury Jn Viaduct	3.24 - 3.30	554 - 544
ce = Gresham Viaduct	3.30 - 3.33	543 - 540
cf = Belinda Rd. Viaduct	3.33 - 3.51	323 - 268
cg = Shakespeare Viaduct	3.51 - 3.54	267 - 263
ch = Hardess St. Viaduct	3.55 - 3.61	262 - 253
ck = Wanless Rd. Viaduct	3.61 - 3.66	252 - 241
cl = Holly Grove Viaduct	4.59 - 4.64	240 - 235
cm = Peckham Rye Viaduct	4.66 - 5.16	199 - 168
cn = Moncrieff Viaduct	5.17 - 5.34	167 - 135
cp = Hospital Viaduct	5.34 - 5.48	831 - 855

Miles from Charing Cross

old Deptford Creek Lift Bridge

DEPTFORD 4.76 GREENWICH 5.35

48 : DLR to Canary Wharf

Greenwich College Tunnel (450 Yds)

48 : DLR to Lewisham

MAZE HILL 6.27

WESTCOMBE PARK 6.76

5 : to Charlton

[SO 290] NKL S : SE

North Kent East Jn

DN GREENWICH UP GREENWICH

BAY OOU D UP DOWN

NEW CROSS SPUR

Rolt St Jn DN NX UP NX

Canal Jn 8.70km

Bricklayers Arms Jn (2.12)

New Cross Gate Depot

Kms from Dalston

Edward St. Jn 4.60

EAST LONDON LINE
46B

NEW CROSS 4.68 (9.90km)

Platforms
A, C ⑫
B ⑩
D ⑤

[SO 130] XTD S : SE

Miles from Charing Cross

Tanners Hill OB 5.18
Lucas Street Tunnels (87 Yds)
Tanners Hill 5.29 Jn
5.22
5.26

ST. JOHNS 5.47 ⑫
5.54

BEX S : SE

48 : DOCKLANDS LIGHT RLY

Lewisham Crossover Jns A-D
A 5.72
B & D 5.78 [7.58]
C 7.53

ø Side 4th rail both lines
z DOWN MID KENT
x UP MID KENT

LEWISHAM 6.04/7.61 (Vic (E))
ø (A) (B) (C) (D)

Vdct 6.07-9
6.10
Courthill Lp Jn Nth 6.21

LCH

'Lewisham OR COURTHILL LOOP'

NCS [SO 130]

[SO 300] [SO 130]
LLL LADYWELL LOOP
S : SE

Parks Bridge Jn

Courthill Lp Jn Sth

Ladywell Jn 6.41 [6.29]

LADYWELL 6.62 ⑫

4 : to Hayes

5 : to Blackheath

3B

ELL
Under construction

ELL
Under Construction

QUEEN'S ROAD PECKHAM 2.58

[SO 680] BTH 1
(2.64)
S : LBSC

NEW CROSS GATE 2.70 (9.62km)
Platforms
2,4,5 ⑧
3 ⑨

[SO 130] LBW S : SE
[SO 510]

(Brockley Lane) 6.60

LBW S : LBSC
[SO 510]

LVT
[SO 130]

St. Johns / Flyover reversible

BR

ST. JOHNS

DOWN NORTH KENT UP NORTH KENT

7.40
7.37

(VS) (L)
Lewisham Vale Jn

NTL [SO 330]
S : LCD-SR

XTD [SO 330]
5.75

= Hatherell Bridge

PECKHAM RYE 5.13

CAT [SO 260] S : LCD

5.48 DOWN CATFORD LOOP
5.32 UP CATFORD LOOP

CAT NTL
CAT
6.10

DOWN LEWISHAM
UP LEWISHAM

BROCKLEY 3.56

4 : to Norwood Jn

4 : to Shortlands

Cow Lane Bridge 3.13

NUNHEAD 5.77

Nunhead Jn
5.32

arches 240 - 201

Vdct

cl cm cn cp

cm cp

P

3.47 3.36 3.28

QUEEN'S ROAD PECKHAM

Future East London Jn
2.25

South Bermondsey Jn 1.49

SOUTH BERMONDSEY 1.63 ⑧

LBC [SO 510]

LBC S : LBSC
[SO 510]

Up Tattenham Crossing (Spa Rd)
Down Tattenham Crossing (Blue Anchor)

Miles from London Bridge

arches 46-54

arches 55-134

Thames Jn

s t

1.60
1.62
2.08 2.15
2.25
2.35
2.45

DOWN SLOW
DOWN FAST
UP SLOW
UP FAST
UP CARR SDG

No. 2 UP CARR SDG

Rolt St Jn

3.09 (10.04km)
3.05
3.57
2.51

Signal Gantries

Up Sigs L148 etc 3.09
Up Sigs L155 etc 3.21

(Southwark Park Stn)

No. 1 DOWN
No. 2 REVERSIBLE
No. 3 UP
No. 4 DOWN
No. 5 DOWN
No. 6 UP

(Blue Anchor)
3.25 3.32
3.39

3.54
3.48 DOWN SLOW 3.48
DOWN FAST
UP FAST

REVERSIBLE
DOWN SOUTH LONDON
UP S LONDON

South Bermondsey Jn 1.49

3.58
a532 a500 a470 a384 a329 4.23 na nb

4.03 3.38 3.48 3.54 4.07 4.06

arches 321-298

nc nd ne nf ng

4.06 4.34 4.38

4.34 4.38

1.63

2 REV 3 UP 6 UP 5 DOWN 4 DOWN

DC AB DF

DOWN SLOW UP SLOW DOWN FAST UP FAST

Up Sigs L140 etc 2.58
Dn Sigs L147 etc 2.70
a680

Dn Sigs L155 etc 3.21

Spa Rd stn site
2.72
2.6 U
PL
*
1.03
1.09
1.00
1.15 1.28
1.20 1.33

[SO 130] XTD S : SE

Spa Rd

LBW [SO 510]
1.60

n 1.00 p q

LBC [SO 510] S : LBSC

1.45
1.59

South Bermondsey Jn 1.49

PECKHAM RYE 5.13

1 ⑩

[HGP 8]
Grove Park Carriage Service Shed

CRIPPLE

B REC 8.20 SHUNT NECK
A RECEPTION

No. 2 WASHER LINE
No. 1 WASHER LINE 8.35

8.15

21
24
28

'St. Mildreds'
'Grove Park Up EMU Sdg'

[HGP 9]

Miles from Charing Cross 9

Pit

No. 2 SIDING
No. 1 SIDING

8.50 8.55

8.40 8.65

CARR. REC.

GROVE PARK 8.78

9.15 (L) (AD) Ashford 9.61

4 5

2 3

BROMLEY N. 9.07
BRANCH PFM RD

Platforms
1 ⑩ (⑧ Networker stock)
2, 4 ⑫
3, 5 ⑩

[SO 130] XTD S : SE

ELMSTEAD WOODS 10.21

Chislehurst Slow Tunnel (649 yds)

10.10 10.10

9.63 10.10

Chislehurst Fast Tunnel (591 yds)

10.63

CHISLEHURST 11.19

DOWN SLOW
UP SLOW

10.77

DOWN FAST
UP FAST

D OOU
10.63

SUNDRIDGE PARK 10.12 ⑩

DOWN
UP

BROMLEY NORTH 10.47

[SO 350] BNG S : SE

(⑧ Networker stock)

6A : to Orpington & St. Mary Cray

3

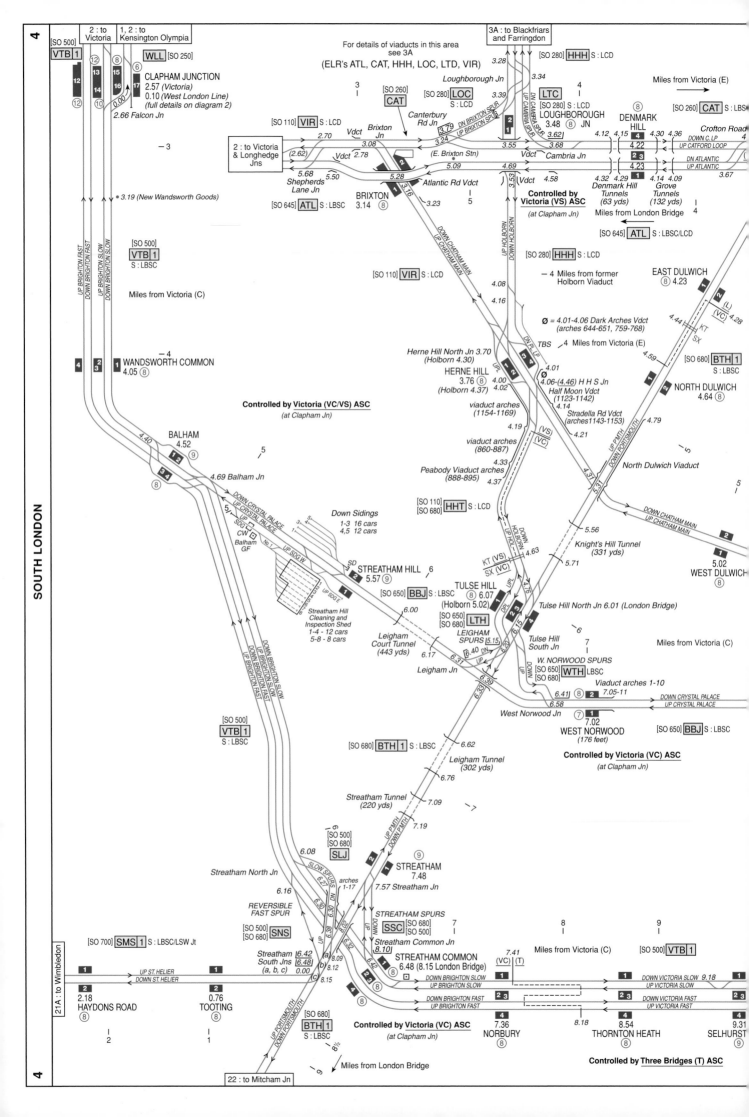

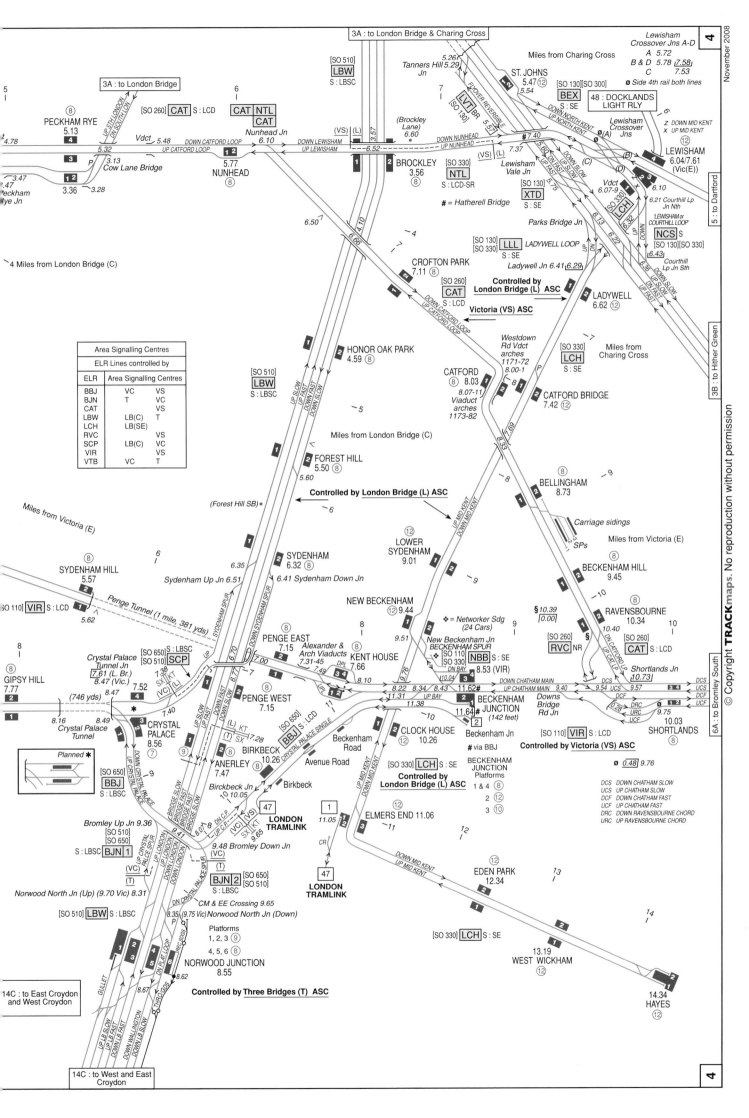

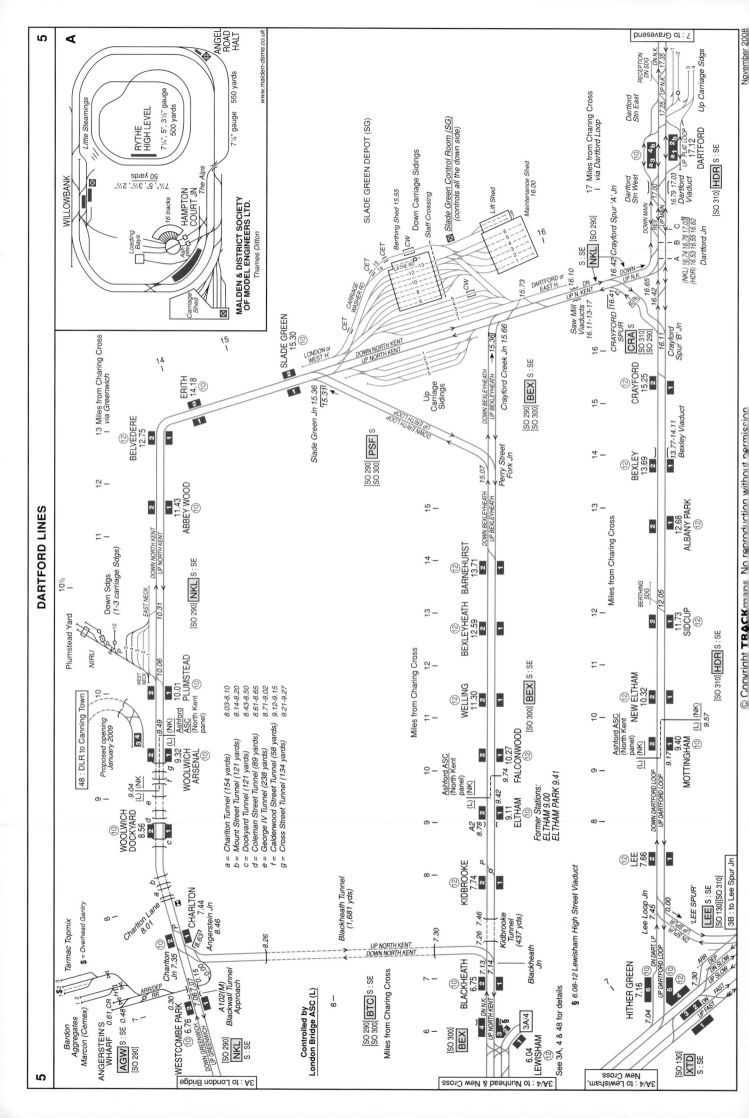

DARTFORD LINES

© Copyright TRACKmaps. No reproduction without permission

November 2008

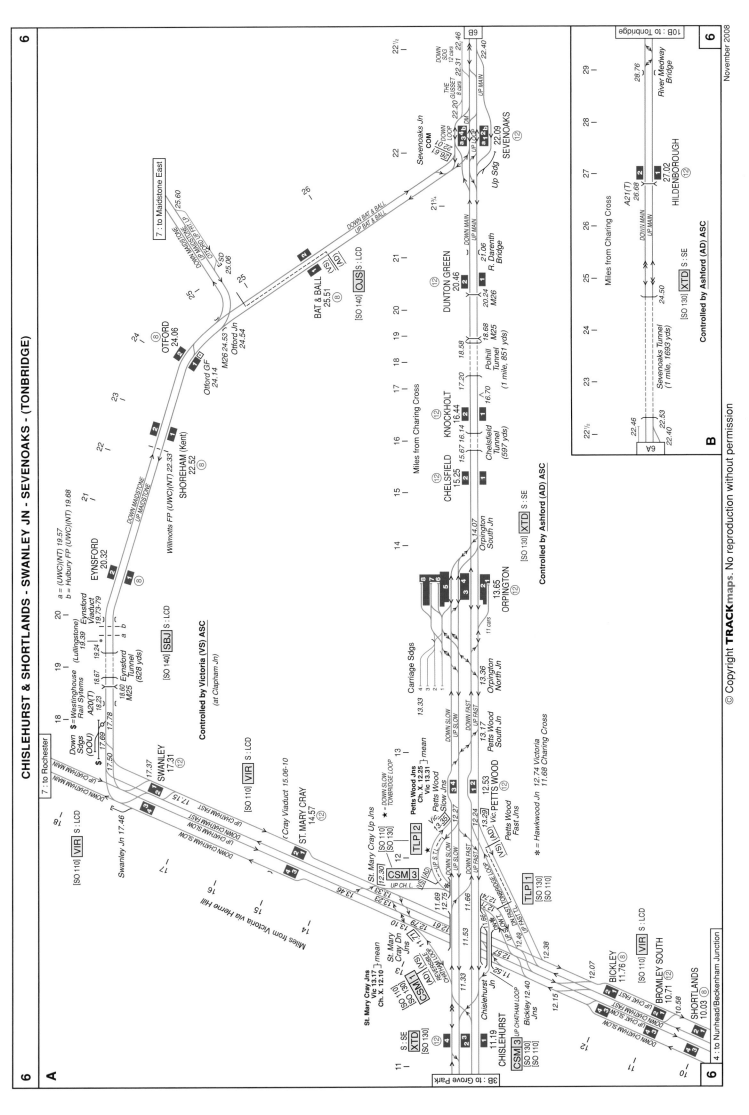

CHISLEHURST & SHORTLANDS - SWANLEY JN - SEVENOAKS - (TONBRIDGE)

November 2008

DARTFORD - STROOD - MAIDSTONE ● SWANLEY - ROCHESTER ● SWANLEY - MAIDSTONE

18   19   20   21   22

49C : CTRL to London, St. Pancras International

Controlled by Ashford (ASC) (North Kent Panel)

5 : to Crayford & Slade Green

Dartford Stn East

RECEPTION DOWN SDG

a3 4 b

17.25   17.35

a1 2 b

UP PLAT. LP
DARTFORD 17.12
⑩

Up Carriage Sdgs

NORTHFLEET 21.67

Springhead Rd 22.42

DOWN NORTH KENT / UP NORTH KENT 17.69

2   (NK) 19.14   2   20.03-15   ⑩   2   21.37   2

Dartford River Crossing Bridge

1   19.07   1   19.69   Greenhithe Tunnel (253 yds)   1   21.17   1

STONE CROSSING ⑫

GREENHITHE for Blue Water ⑩

SWANSCOMBE

[SO 310] HDR S : SE

Sprin Jn (U 22.27 37.37

22.21

Sprin Jn (U 22.27

49C : CTRL to Ebbsfleet

49C : to Ebbsfleet & London St Pancras Intl.

⑩

EBBSFLEET (See 49C)

CTRL controlled by Ashford (AF) (ASC)

Distances in kilometres

Former FJS Fawkham Jn to Gravesend West

49D : Southfleet Jn CTRL etc.

205
204
203
202
201

DC/AC changeover   DOWN WATERLOO CONNECTION NIRU / UP WATERLOO CONNECTION NIRU

202.170km

Boundaries:
Track KT 200.335km CTRI
Signalling Down KT 202.114km CTRI
Up CTRL 202.543km KT

201.308km

18   19   20   21   22   23   24   25   26

⑫
SWANLEY 17.31

FARNINGHAM ROAD 20.42

200.091km

MEOPHAM 25.76

17.46

3 4

NIRU NIRU

2   2   2

1 2

17.37   Swanley Jn

17.50

19.20 M25

1   20.68-74 Darenth Viaduct   Fawkham Jn 22.50   1   (VS) (ER)   1

⑧

1   23.30 **LONGFIELD** ⑫

24.38

⑫

Westinghouse Rail Sytems

Controlled by Victoria (VS) ASC

(at Clapham Jn)

DOWN SDGS

17.78

— 18

18.23) (A20(T)

Eynsford Tunnel (828 yds) 19.24

18.67 —18.60 M25

— 19

19.39 (Lullingstone)

(UWC)(NT) 19.57

Eynsford Vdct.) 19.73-79

Hulbury FP (UWC)(NT) —20

1   2 **EYNSFORD** 20.32 ⑧

— 21

[SO 140] SBJ S : LCD

UP MAIDSTONE / DOWN MAIDSTONE

— 22

22.33 — Willmotts FP (UWC)(NT)

1   2 **SHOREHAM (Kent)** 22.52 ⑧

— 23

6A : to St Mary Cray

6A : to Bat & Ball & Sevenoaks

GRAIN

Miles from Charing Cross *via Dartford Loop*

34   35   36   37   38

To Hoo Jn : see top right

GRAIN 38.41

Marcroft Engineering

(Beluncle)

GRAIN 34.15 BRANCH

34.57 (Kingsnorth Whitehall Sdgs GF)

(Middle Stoke) 36.25   (Stoke Jn) 37.01

a b

36.74 (Stoke Jn Halt)

c d e f g h

37.79-38.00 Yantlet Flood gate

Grain Crossing (UWC)(NT) 38.22

38.26 NR EWS DOWN SDG

I Grain Crossing Halt 38.24

UP / DN

38.48   BP 'B' Gate   Foster Yeoman

WEIGHBRIDGE   MIDDLE CEMENT

WB

Spoil unloading Sdg

Stone loading area

Pad   BP Sidings (3-7)

Bitumen Terminal

Thamesport (open)

Isle of Grain Depot Foster Yeoman Quarries Ltd

WB

Thamesport Freightliner Terminal

overhead travelling cranes

Thamesport Bulk Terminal Hutchison Whampoa

(to former Port Victoria 39.51)

River Medway

Controlled by Ashford (ASC) (North Kent Panel) (NK)

[SO 320] HTG S : SE

a = Jacobs No. 1 (UWC) 35.25
b = Stoke Creek (UWC) 35.64
c = Recreation (UWC) 36.20
d = Middle Stoke (UWC) 36.25
e = Muggeridge (UWC) 36.33
f = Wick No. 1 (UWC) 36.56
g = Stoke (ABCL) 36.77
h = Chalkwalk (UWC) 37.38

— 24

1   2 **OTFORD** 24.06 ⑧

Otford GF 24.14

— 25

M26 24.53)

Otford Jn 24.53

26   27   28   29   30   31   32   33

Miles from Victoria *via Herne Hill*

UP B&B / DN B&B

DOWN MAIDSTONE / UP MAIDSTONE

26.18

OTFORD UP GDS LP 25.60

SD

25.06

Seal (UWC) 25.78

2   DN PASS. LOOP   ENGRS'   2

28.66   29.38

1   (VS) (ME)   1

26.79 **KEMSING** ⑥

28.16

29.53 **BOROUGH GREEN & WROTHAM** ⑧

[SO 140] SBJ S : LCD

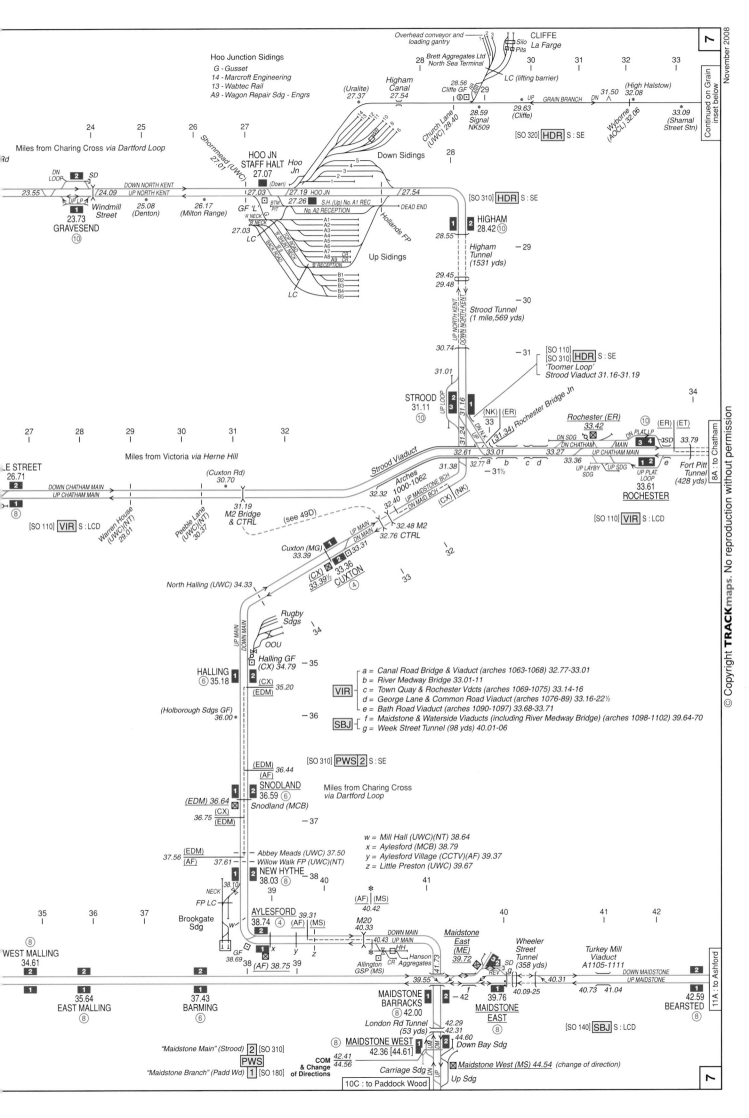

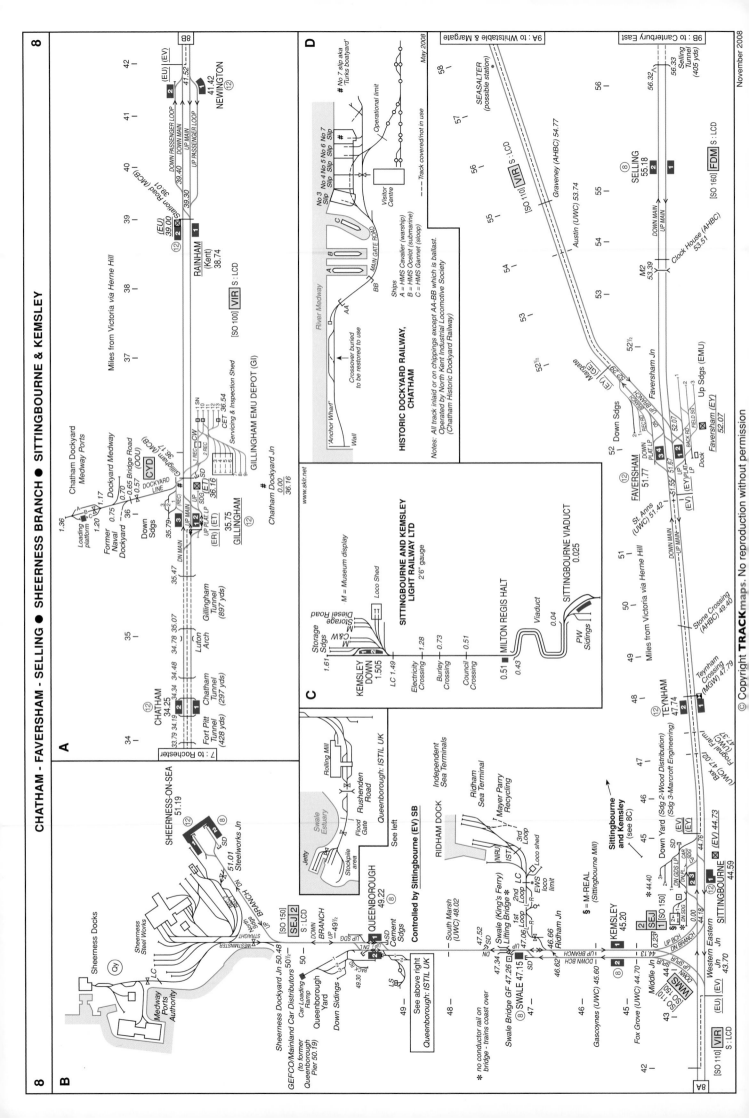

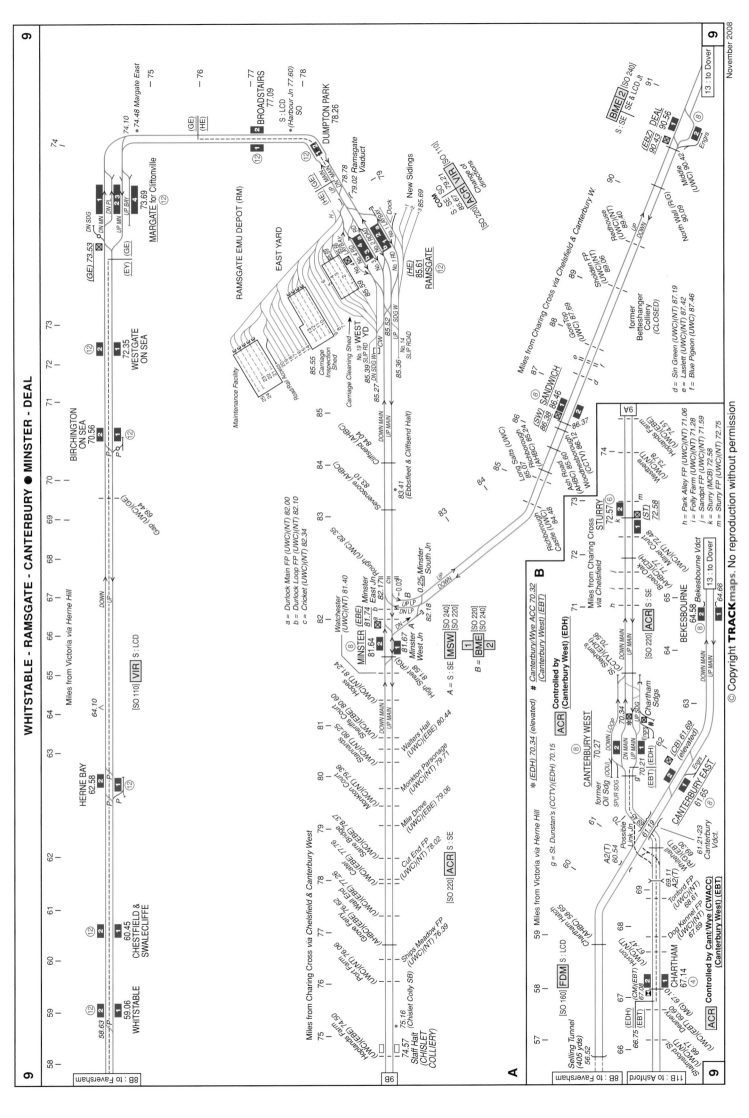

November 2008

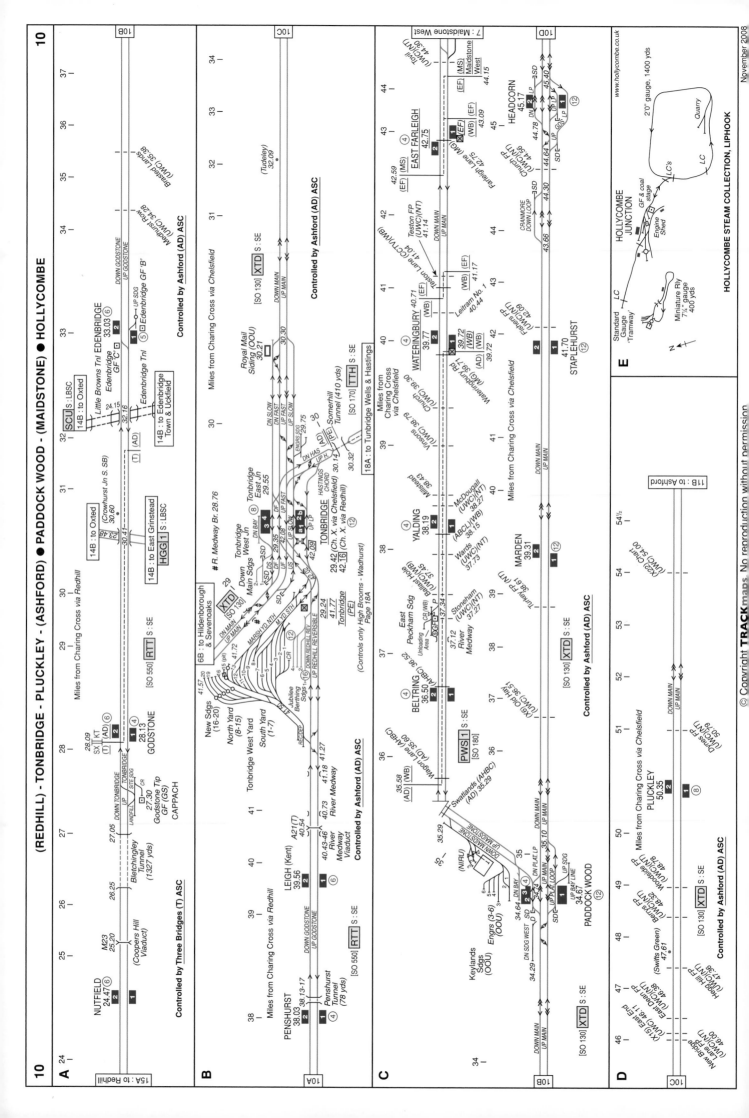

(REDHILL) - TONBRIDGE - PLUCKLEY - (ASHFORD) ● PADDOCK WOOD - (MAIDSTONE) ● HOLLYCOMBE

November 2008

HOLLYCOMBE STEAM COLLECTION, LIPHOOK

www.hollycombe.co.uk

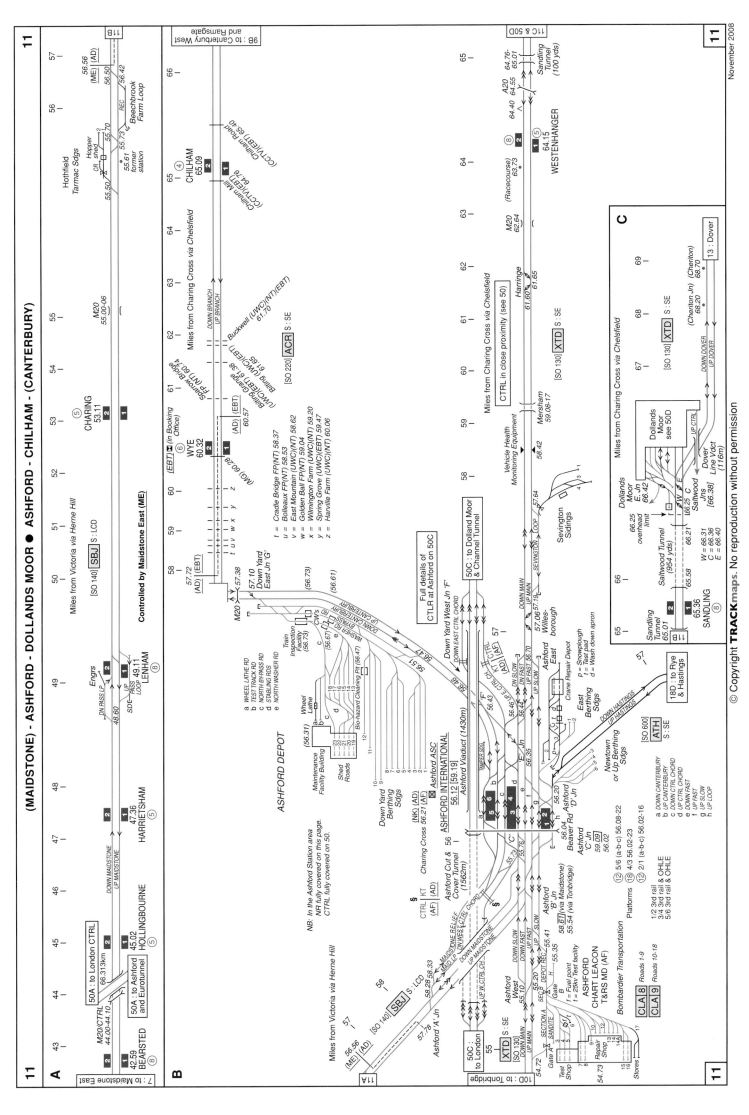

(MAIDSTONE) - ASHFORD - DOLLANDS MOOR ● ASHFORD - CHILHAM - (CANTERBURY)

© Copyright TRACKmaps. No reproduction without permission

November 2008

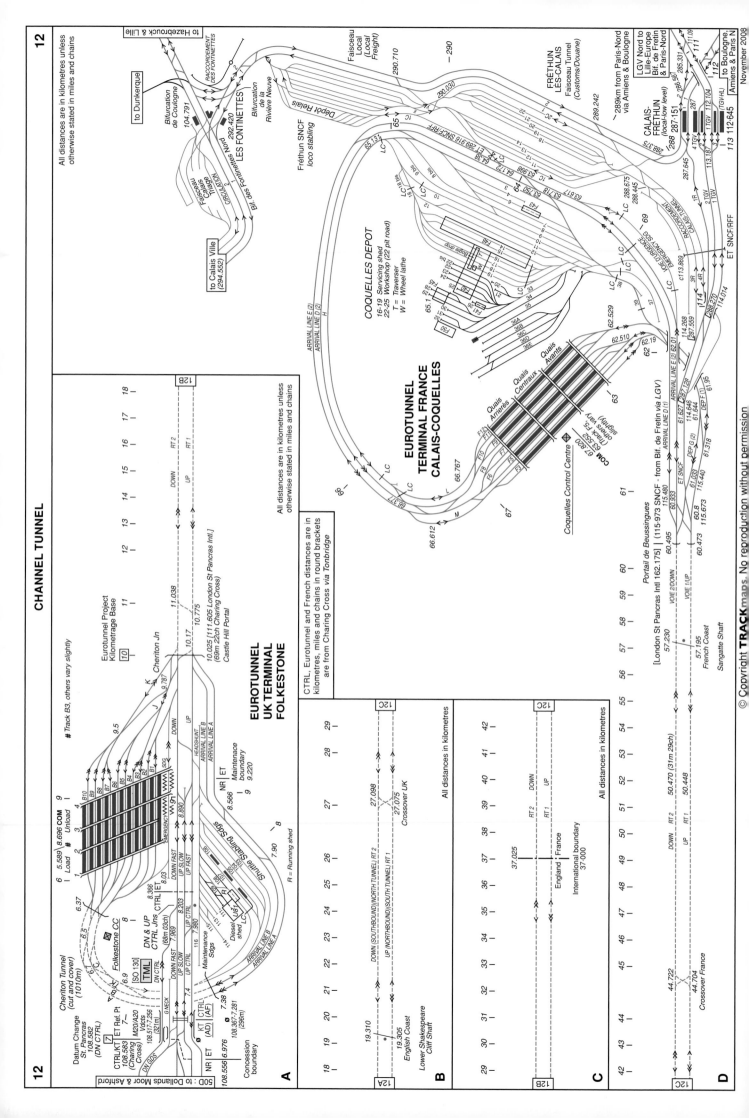

CHANNEL TUNNEL

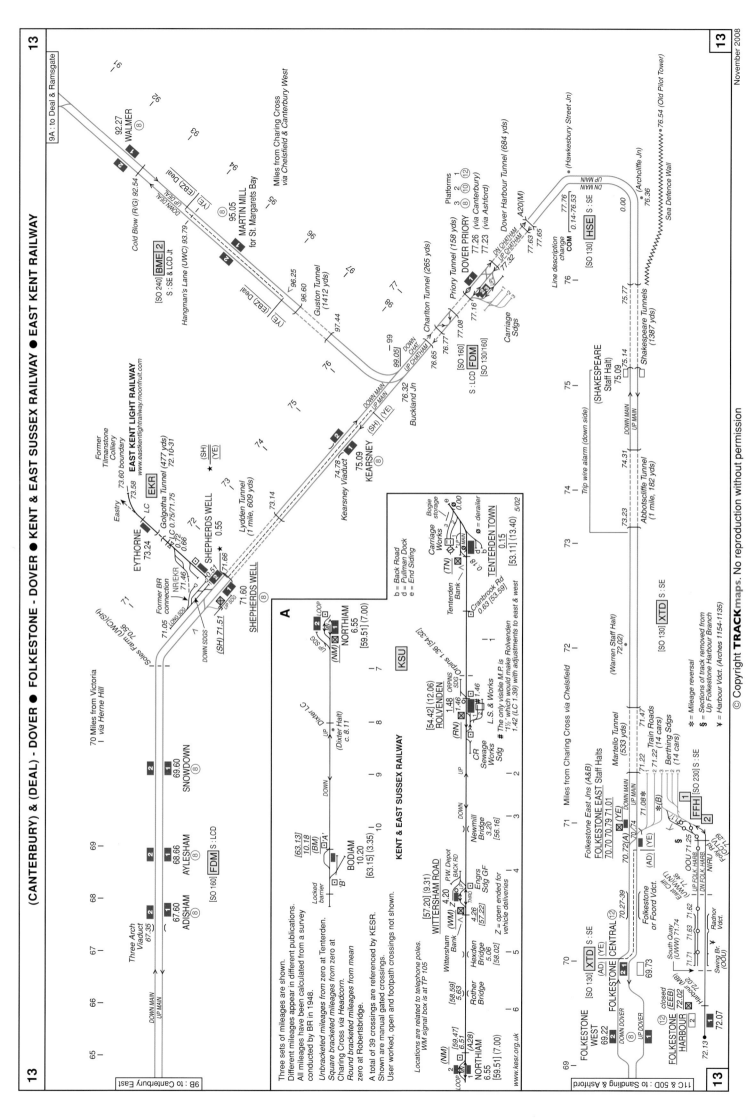

(CANTERBURY) & (DEAL) - DOVER ● FOLKESTONE - DOVER ● KENT & EAST SUSSEX RAILWAY ● EAST KENT RAILWAY

November 2008

9A : to Deal & Ramsgate

9B : to Canterbury East

11C & SDD : to Sandling & Ashford

WALMER 92.27

MARTIN MILL 95.05 for St. Margarets Bay

Cold Blow (R/G) 92.54

Hangman's Lane (UWC) 93.79

[SO 240] BME 2 — S : SE & LCD Jt

DOWN DEAL UP DEAL (EB2) Deal (YE) (EB2) Deal (YE)

Miles from Charing Cross via Chelsfield & Canterbury West

Guston Tunnel (1412 yds)

Chariton Tunnel (265 yds)

Priory Tunnel (158 yds)

DOVER PRIORY 77.26 (via Canterbury) 77.23 (via Ashford)

Platforms 3 (8) (10) (12) 2 1

[SO 160] FDM — S : LCD [SO 130/160]

Carriage Sdgs

A20(M)

DN CHATHAM UP CHATHAM 77.32

77.16 77.08

76.77 76.65

DOWN CHAT UP CHATHAM 99.05

Buckland Jn 76.32

DOWN MAIN UP MAIN (SH) (YE)

KEARSNEY 75.09 (8)

Kearsney Viaduct 74.78

Lydden Tunnel (1 mile, 609 yds)

(SH) (YE) 73.14

EAST KENT LIGHT RAILWAY www.eastkentlightrailway.moonfruit.com

Former Tilmanstone Colliery

Eastry 73.60 boundary

EKR

EYTHORNE 73.24

Golgotha Tunnel (477 yds) 72.10-31 73.58 LC

Former BR connection

NR/EKR 71.46

SHEPHERDS WELL 0.55 0.66 0.72

SHEPHERDS WELL (8) 71.66 2.57 71.60 71.51 (SH)

LONG SDG UP SDG DOWN SDGS

Sokes Farm (UWC)(SH) 70.96

71.05

70 Miles from Victoria via Herne Hill

Three Arch Viaduct 67.35

ADISHAM 67.60 (8) 2 1

AYLESHAM 68.66 (8) 2 1

SNOWDOWN 69.60 (8) 2 1

[SO 160] FDM — S : LCD

KENT & EAST SUSSEX RAILWAY

www.kesr.org.uk

(NM) NORTHIAM 6.55 2 [59.51] (7.00) [59.47] 6.51 (A28) LOOP

Wittersham Bank

Rother Bridge [58.59] 5.63

Hexden Bridge 5.06 [58.02]

WITTERSHAM ROAD [57.20] (9.31) (WM) Z 4.20 4.26 [57.22] Engrs Sdg GF

Locked barrier 'A' 'B' BACK RD THRO P.W. Depot

BODIAM 10.20 [63.15] (3.35) [63.13] 10.18 (BM)

NORTHIAM 6.55 (NM) 2 1 6.55 [59.51] (7.00)

Newmill Bridge 3.20 [56.16]

Dixter LC

(Dixter Halt) c. 8.11

DOWN UP

b = Back Road
d = Pullman Dock
e = End Siding

Carriage Works Bogie storage

TENTERDEN TOWN 0.15 [53.11] (13.40) 0.00

(TN) ⊗ MAIN UP 3 2 1 e d b 5/02

Tenterden Bank

Cranbrook Rd 0.63 [53.56]

⊗ = derailer

ROLVENDEN [54.42] (12.06) 1.48 1.46 (RN) ORPINS SDG

L.S. & Works

CR Sewage Works Sdg

The only visible M.P. is '1½' which would make Rolvenden 1.42 (LC 1.39) with adjustments to east & west

KSU

A

Miles from Charing Cross via Chelsfield

(Hawkesbury Street Jn) *76.54 (Old Pilot Tower)

(Archcliffe Jn) 76.36

Line description change COM 0.14-76.53 77.76-76.53

HSE — S : SE [SO 130]

DN MAIN UP MAIN 77.65 77.63 0.00

Dover Harbour Tunnel (684 yds)

Sea Defence Wall

Shakespeare Tunnels (1387 yds)

75.77 75.14 75.09

(SHAKESPEARE Staff Halt)

DOWN MAIN UP MAIN 74.31

Trip wire alarm (down side)

Abbottscliffe Tunnel (1 mile, 182 yds)

73.23

[SO 130] XTD — S : SE

72 (Warren Staff Halt) 72.02

Miles from Charing Cross via Chelsfield

Martello Tunnel (533 yds)

Folkestone East Jns (A&B)

FOLKESTONE EAST Staff Halts 70.70 70.79 71.01

70.72(A) (YE) 70.74

(AD) (YE)

Train Roads (14 cars) 71.47 71.22

Berthing Sdgs (14 cars) 71.22

71.08 *(B)

§ FFH [SO 230] S : SE 1 2

OOU 71.25

OOU 71.63 UP FOLK HARB DN FOLK HARB

South Quay (UWW) 71.62 71.71 71.63

Folkestone or Foord Vdct. 70.27-39

East Cliff (UWW)(UNI) 71.46

[SO 130] XTD — S : SE

FOLKESTONE WEST 69.22 (8)

DOWN DOVER UP DOVER

(AD) (YE)

FOLKESTONE CENTRAL (12) 2 1 69.73

Radnor Vdct.

Swing Br (OOU)

FOLKESTONE HARBOUR 72.02 (12) closed 2 1 72.07 72.13

Harbour Vdct. (MB)

* = Mileage reversal
* = Sections of track removed from Up Folkestone Harbour Branch
§
¥ = Harbour Vdct. (Arches 1154-1135)

A

Miles from London Bridge *via Oxted*

39   40   41   42   43   44   45   46

Crowborough Jn
14B
38.73

Engineers' Sdgs

39.40

39.61

DOWN UCKFIELD
39.25   UP UCKFIELD

Switch Control Panel

39.45

39.11
CROWBOROUGH
⑦

2   **1**

40.27   *Crowborough Tunnel*
(1022 yds)

41.63-70
Sleeches Viaduct

Greenhurst Jn
42.53

42.64-69
Greenhurst Viaduct

'UCKFIELD SINGLE'

④ BUXTED
43.68
UP   DN
43.70

44.00

45.10
45.00

45.14
Hempstead (UWC)

46.08 UCKFIELD
⑧

1 SCU 2

[SO 540] SCU 1   S : LBSC

Controlled by Oxted (OD) SB

B

[SO 540] SCU 1   S : LBSC

25   26   27   28   29   30   31   32

Miles from London Bridge

10A : to Tonbridge

Edenbridge Tnl
197 yds

⑥ **2**   ⑥ **2**   *Hever Jn* 27.42

Little Browns Tnl 121 yds

24.15

24.15   24.10

Mark Beech Tunnel
(1341 yds)

28.26   29.07   ⑥ COWDEN 29.26

Blackham Jn 31.14
DN

UP 'UCKFIELD SINGLE'

31.69
AS...

1   EDENBRIDGE TOWN 25.47

1   HEVER 27.27

River Medway

Controlled by

20   21   22   23

RTT
S : SE

10A : to Tonbridge

32.16   10A : to Tonbridge

DOWN UCKFIELD   UP UCKFIELD

23

S : SE RTT

24   25   26   27

Miles from London Bridge

14C
DN EAST GRINS'D
UP EAST GRINS'D

④ DOWN BAY
(OD) 20.32
20.40-46   20.58

2 3

⑫ **1** UP SDG
LONG DOCK   *Oxted Vdct*
20.25
OXTED

21.03

Limpsfield Tunnel
(565 yds)

2

1 21.35 *Hurst Green Jn*
21.20
HURST GREEN
⑫

*Sunt Farm No. 1
(UWC) 23.23*

30.41

23.48

10A : to Redhill

Lingfield
26.17 **2** FP Racecourse 26.28

DOWN EAST GRINSTEAD
UP EAST GRINSTEAD

1
26.23
LINGFIELD
⑧

[SO 530] SCU 1   S : LBSC & SE Jt

[SO 530] HGG 1
S : LBSC & SE Jt | LBSC
(Crowhurst Jn N.)

C

**NB : Distances and layouts distorted in the
Norwood Junction/Selhurst and Windmill Jn area**

Miles from London Bridge

[SO 510/500] LBW
[SO 500] **1 VTB 2**
COM   [SO 500]

9   10

EAST
F

6 DO...
5 SLO...
4 UP S...
3 DOW...
2 FAS...
1 UP ...

NORWOOD JUNCTION
8.55 (170 feet) 8.62

4 : to Crystal Palace/Sydenham

REC SDG

6

DOWN LB SLOW
8.67 West Croydon Jn

4 5

2 3

1

Platforms
⑨ 1-3
⑧ 4-6

(OOU) 8.72
DN PLAT LOOP

Tennison Rd 8.79

9.05

9.19

THRO' ROAD / GOODS ROAD
DOWN LONDON BRIDGE SLOW
DOWN WALLINGTON

9.22

DOWN LONDON BRIDGE FAST
UP LONDON BRIDGE FAST
UP LONDON BRIDGE SLOW
FORK ARRIVAL ROAD

8.79   DEPARTURE ROAD
ARRIVAL ROAD

GULLET
No. 1 YARD RD
No. 2 YARD RD
Toilet aprons

WASHER ROAD

CW

Fork Intersection Bridge

9.26

Norwood Fork Jns
9.30

9.33   9.35
SELHURST SUBSTATION SDG

(NIRU) 9.39

9.38

9.25 P 9.26
OOU

CW

[SO 500] LBW
[SO 510]   S : LBSC

'Perturbation Sdg'
9.45

9.55 SD

Cottage Bridge
DOWN LONDON BRIDGE FAST
UP LONDON BRIDGE FAST
UP LONDON BRIDGE SLOW

Windmill Bridge Jn
9.69 LB →
10.03 Vic

(9.61 LB)   DOWN SLOW
UP SLOW

9.68   (LB) 9.68   DOWN FAST
UP FAST

(9.76 Vic)   9.43   FAST 10.10
UP SDG

10.02 9.72
(Vic)

REVERSIBL

Cottage Jn
9.52 LB
9.67 Vic

[SO 510] NFE   S : LBSC
DOWN WALLINGTON
UP WALLINGTON

AC: 25kv Test Compound

9.58

Lupin Intersection Bridge

9.40

DOWN VICTORIA SLOW
UP VICTORIA SLOW

Field Sidings

DOWN S.S.
UP S.S.
UP SELHURST SPUR

9.60

9.46
Selhurst Jn
S : LBSC

§

*Gloucester Intersection Bridge
Gloucester Road Jn*
9.49 LB →
9.66 Vic]

(St James Jn)
Vic 9.72, LB 9.61

§
[SO 510]
[SO 500]
WCS
S : LBSC

(Selhurst Depot 'S')

Fuelling Points

No. 1 ACCESS
No. 2 ACCESS

New Inspection Shed
No. 3 NEW
RR

1 ... 3 ... AC

Control Desk

Chalk Sdgs

5 4 3

DEP ROAD
AFR ROAD
NEW No.2

NEW No.1

ARRIVAL ROAD
DEPARTURE ROAD

DOWN VICTORIA SLOW
UP VICTORIA SLOW

DOWN VICTORIA FAST
UP VICTORIA FAST

[SO 500] **VTB 1** S : LBSC

NB: Only 3 chains between Selhurst Junctions

OAKFIELD SDG

DOWN WALLINGTON
UP WALLINGTON

West Croydon

SELHURST DEPOT (SU)
NYD

AC Sidings
*Servicing areas
between
AC1/2, 2/3 etc*

(16a Wheel Lathe)

14 16 17
15 16a 18 19

Repair Shop

1 2 3 4   5 6 7 8

North Sidings
9.32

*Inspection and
Cleaning Shed
(former DC Shed)*

9.46
1

9.18
2 3

9.37 *Selhurst Jn*
4
9.31
SELHURST

DOWN VICTORIA SLOW
UP VICTORIA SLOW
DOWN VICTORIA FAST
UP VICTORIA FAST

9.43

⑧
WEST CROYDON
10.35
(179 feet)
10.37

UP BAY

1 3   **4**

Centrale

[SO 510] NFE
S : LBSC

Miles from Victoria

4 : to Streatham Common & Clapham Junction

22 : to Sutton

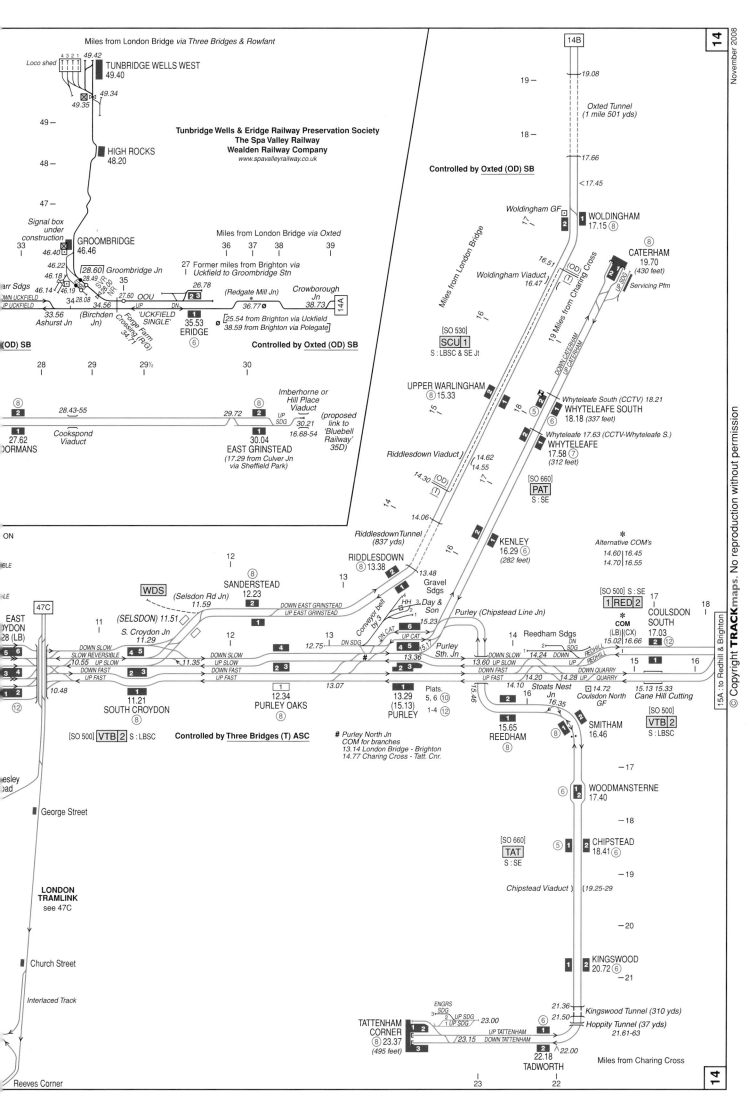

November 2008

Miles from London Bridge *via Three Bridges & Rowfant*

Loco shed 4 3 2 1 *49.42*
TUNBRIDGE WELLS WEST
49.40

49.34
49.35

49 —

HIGH ROCKS
48.20

48 —

47 —

Tunbridge Wells & Eridge Railway Preservation Society
The Spa Valley Railway
Wealden Railway Company
www.spavalleyrailway.co.uk

Signal box under construction
33
GROOMBRIDGE
46.40
46.46

Miles from London Bridge *via Oxted*

36   37   38   39

46.22
46.18
[28.60] *Groombridge Jn*
27 Former miles from Brighton *via Uckfield to Groombridge Stn*

arr Sdgs
46.14
46.19
28.49
SVR
28.00
NR
35

26.78
Crowborough Jn
38.73

34 28.08
34.56
27.60 OOU
UP DN
(Redgate Mill Jn)

2 3

14A

DOWN UCKFIELD
UP UCKFIELD
33.56
(Birchden Jn)
Forge Farm Crossing (R/G) 34.71
'UCKFIELD SINGLE'
1
35.53
ERIDGE
6

[25.54 from Brighton *via Uckfield*
38.59 from Brighton *via Polegate*]

Ashurst Jn

(OD) SB

Controlled by Oxted (OD) SB

28   29   29½   30

8
2
28.43-55
29.72

Imberhorne or Hill Place Viaduct

8
2
UP SDG
30.21
16.68-54

(proposed link to 'Bluebell Railway' 35D)

1
27.62
Cookspond Viaduct

1
30.04
EAST GRINSTEAD
(17.29 from Culver Jn via Sheffield Park)

ORMANS

14B

19 —
19.08

18 —

Oxted Tunnel (1 mile 501 yds)

17.66
<*17.45*

Controlled by Oxted (OD) SB

Woldingham GF
17
1
2
WOLDINGHAM
17.15 8

8
CATERHAM
19.70
(430 feet)
1
2
UP SDG
Servicing Pfm

16.51
(OD)
(T)

Woldingham Viaduct
16.47

[SO 530]
SCU 1
S : LBSC & SE Jt

16

Miles from London Bridge
19 Miles from Charing Cross

DOWN CATERHAM
UP CATERHAM

UPPER WARLINGHAM
8 15.33
2

18
2
1
5
1
2
Whyteleafe South (CCTV) 18.21
WHYTELEAFE SOUTH
18.18 6
(337 feet)

15

Riddlesdown Viaduct)

2
1
Whyteleafe 17.63 (CCTV-Whyteleafe S.)
WHYTELEAFE
17.58 7
(312 feet)

14.62
14.55

[SO 660]
PAT
S : SE

14.30 (OD)
(T)

14.06

2
KENLEY
16.29 6
(282 feet)

*
Alternative COM's
14.60 | 16.45
14.70 | 16.55

RiddlesdownTunnel (837 yds)

RIDDLESDOWN
8 13.38

2
1
13.48 Gravel Sdgs

12

SANDERSTEAD
12.23

13

WDS
(Selsdon Rd Jn)
11.59

8
2
DOWN EAST GRINSTEAD
UP EAST GRINSTEAD

1
Day & Son

4 5
6
15.23

Purley (Chipstead Line Jn)

14
Reedham Sdgs
DN SDG

[SO 500] S : SE
1 RED 2

17
COULSDON SOUTH
17.03 12

18

(SELSDON) 11.51

S. Croydon Jn
11.29

12

1

13
12.75

3 HH
B 1
DN SDG

Conveyor belt by 3
DN CAT
UP CAT

Purley Sth. Jn

DOWN SLOW
UP SLOW
13.60

DOWN SLOW
UP
14.24
REDHILL
REDHILL
DOWN
15.02 16.66

COM
(LB) (CX)

*
EAST CROYDON
28 (LB)

5 6

47C

DOWN SLOW
SLOW REVERSIBLE
10.55 *UP SLOW*

4 5

DOWN SLOW
UP SLOW

DOWN SLOW
UP SLOW

14
15
16

3 4

10.10
11.35

DOWN FAST
UP FAST

DOWN FAST
UP FAST

2 3

1 2

10.48

1
12.34
PURLEY OAKS
8

13.07

1
13.29
(15.13)
PURLEY

Plats. 5, 6 10
1-4 12

DOWN FAST
UP FAST
14.20

DOWN QUARRY
UP QUARRY
14.28

REDHILL
QUARRY

15.13 15.33
Cane Hill Cutting

16

12

SOUTH CROYDON
8

[SO 500] VTB 2 S : LBSC

Controlled by Three Bridges (T) ASC

Purley North Jn
COM for branches
13.14 London Bridge - Brighton
14.77 Charing Cross - Tatt. Cnr.

2
Stoats Nest Jn
14.10
16.35

1
15.65
REEDHAM
8

16
□ *14.72*
Coulsdon North GF

2
1
7
SMITHAM
16.46
8

[SO 500] VTB 2 S : LBSC

esley ad
■ George Street

15.46

— 17

6
1 2
WOODMANSTERNE
17.40

LONDON TRAMLINK
see 47C

— 18

[SO 660]
TAT
S : SE

5 1
2
CHIPSTEAD
18.41 6

— 19

Chipstead Viaduct)   (19.25-29

— 20

■ Church Street

1
2
KINGSWOOD
20.72 6

— 21

Interlaced Track

21.36
21.50
Kingswood Tunnel (310 yds)
Hoppity Tunnel (37 yds)
21.61-63

ENGRS SDG
3
2 UP SDG
1 UP SDG
23.00

6
1

TATTENHAM CORNER
1 2
8 23.37
(495 feet)
3

UP TATTENHAM
23.15 DOWN TATTENHAM

^ *22.00*

2
22.18
TADWORTH

Miles from Charing Cross

Reeves Corner

23   22

15A : to Redhill & Brighton

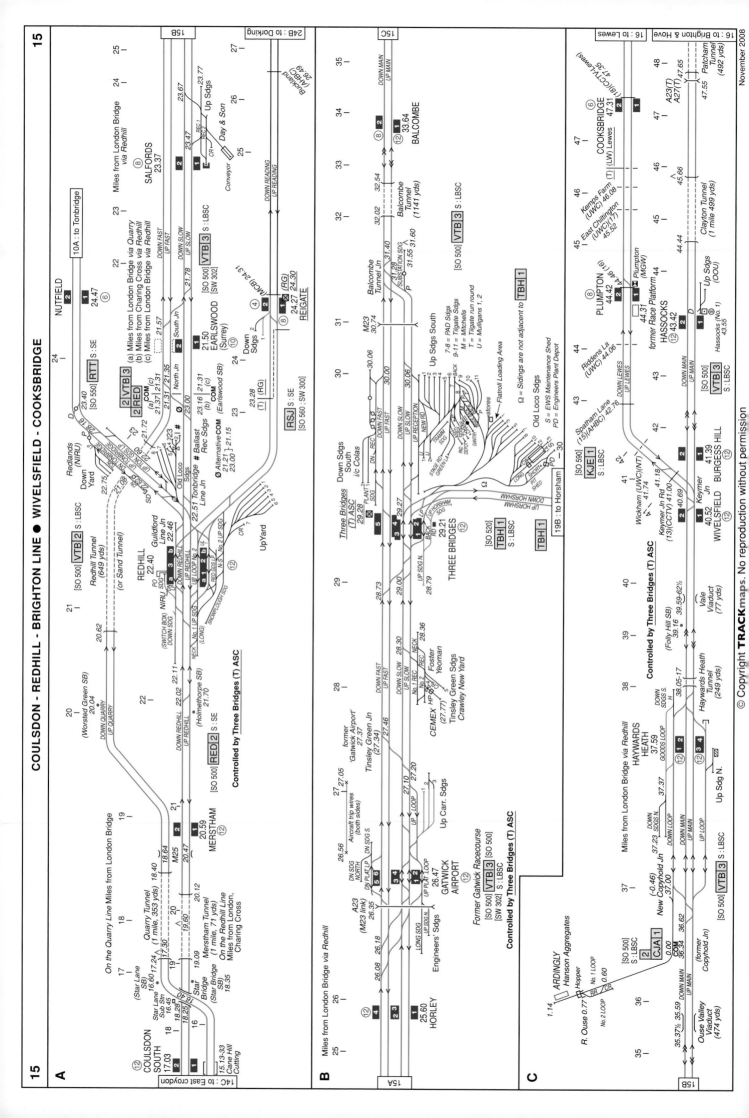

November 2008

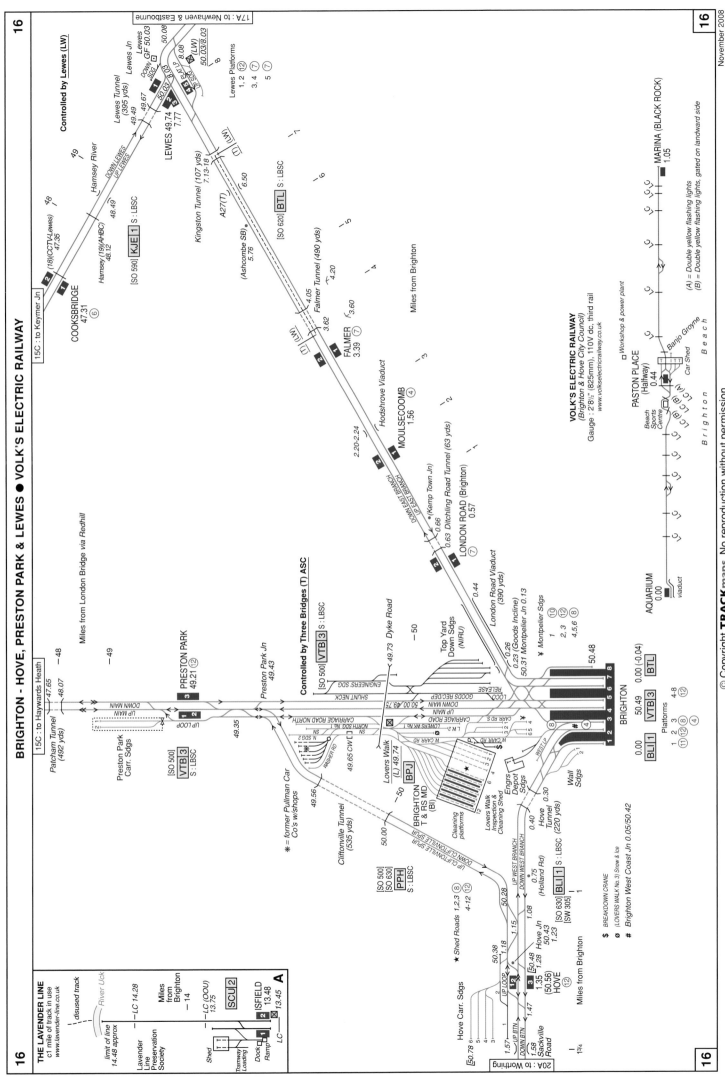

BRIGHTON - HOVE, PRESTON PARK & LEWES ● VOLK'S ELECTRIC RAILWAY

© Copyright **TRACKmaps**. No reproduction without permission

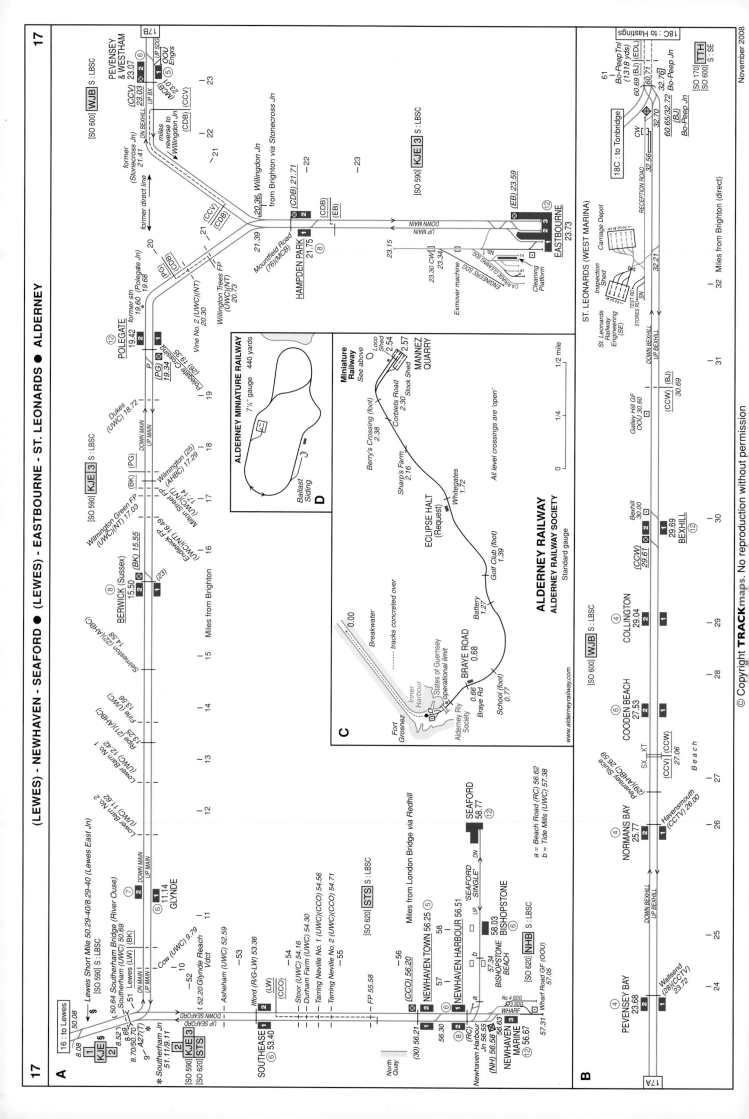

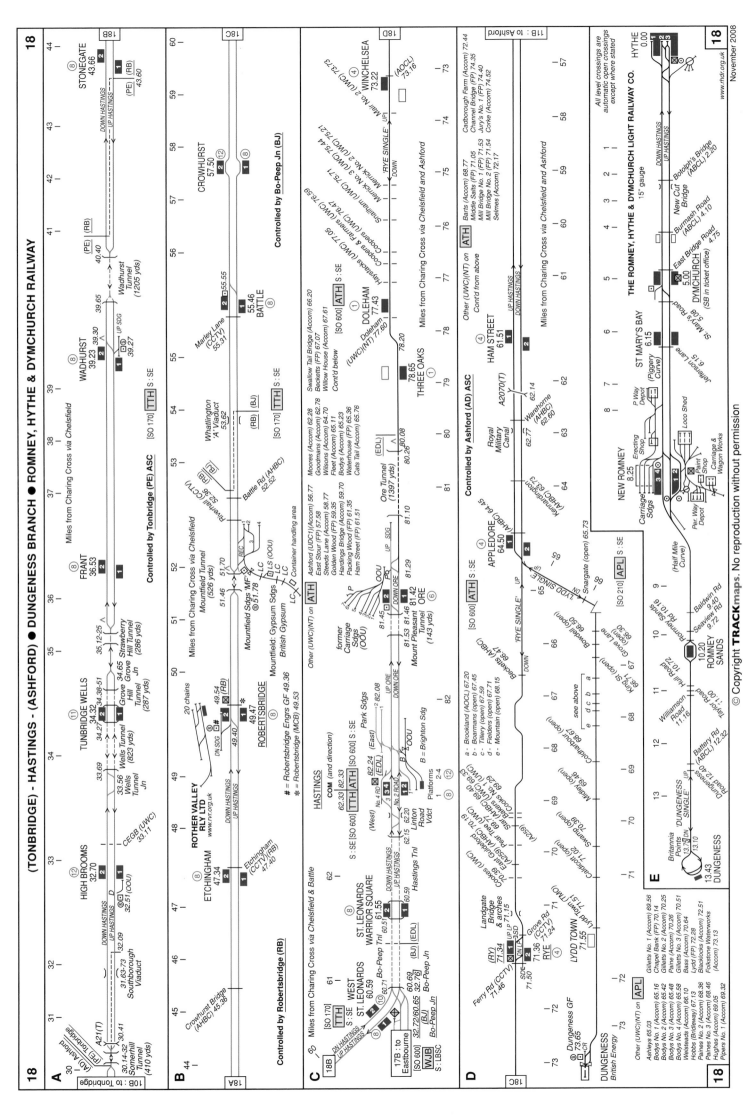

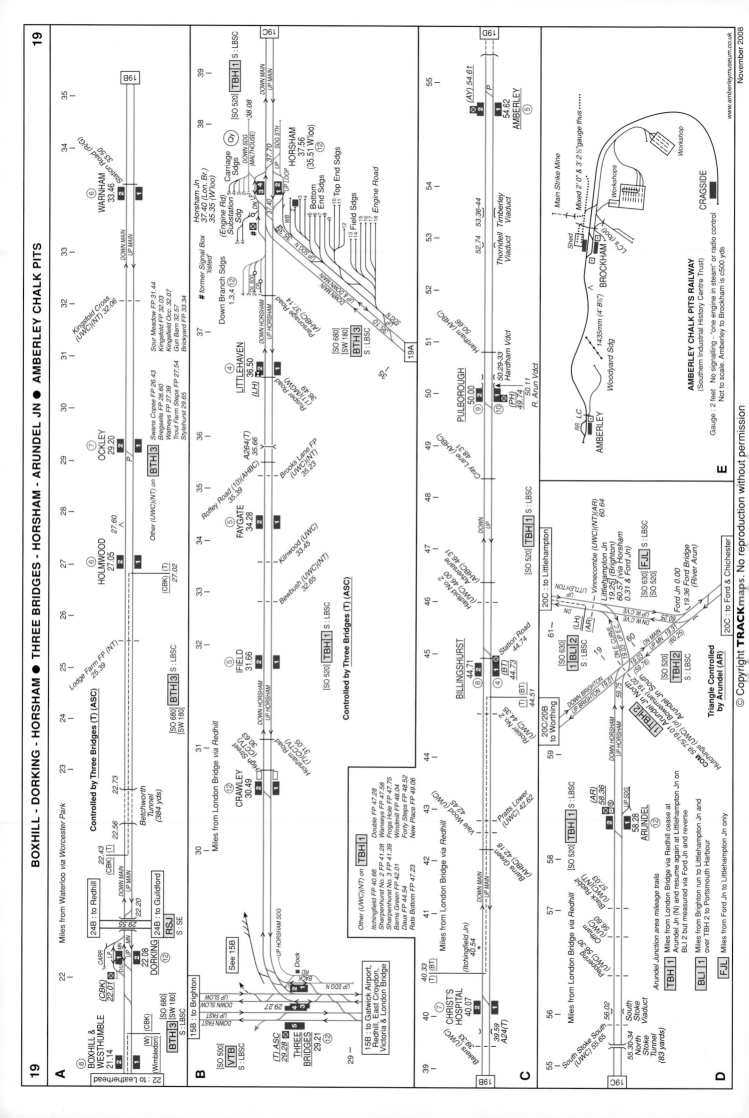

Panel A

Miles from Waterloo via Worcester Park

⑧ BOXHILL & WESTHUMBLE 21.14
(W) [Wimbledon]
[SO 680] [SW 180]
BTH 3 S : LBSC
(CBK) 22.01
CARR
(T) 22.08
DORKING (12)
[SO 680] [SW 180]
24B : to Redhill
24B : to Guildford
RSJ S : SE
22.20
29.55 / 22.20
(CBK) (T) 22.43
22.56
22.73
Betchworth Tunnel (384 yds)
Lodge Farm FP (NT) 25.39
DOWN MAIN / UP MAIN
⑥ WARNHAM 33.46
Station Road (R/G) 33.50
⑥ HOLMWOOD 27.05
27.60
(CBK) (T) 27.02
⑦ OCKLEY 29.20
P
BTH 3
Swans Copse FP 26.43
Bregsells FP 26.60
Watneys FP 27.39
Trout Farm Steps FP 27.54
Stylehurst 29.65
Kingsfold Cross (UWC)(NT) 32.06
Sour Meadow FP 31.44
Kingsfold FP 32.03
Kingsfold Occ. 32.07
Gun Barn 32.57
Brickyard FP 33.34
19B

Panel B

15B : to Brighton
15B : to Gatwick Airport, Redhill, East Croydon, Victoria & London Bridge
[SO 500] VTB S : LBSC
(T) ASC 29.28
THREE BRIDGES (12) 29.21
DOWN FAST / UP FAST
DOWN SLOW / UP SLOW
29.27
BACK RD
Dock
UP SDG N
UP HORSHAM SDG
See 15B
Bakers (UWC) 33.55
Horsham Road (T)(CTV) 31.05
Crawley High Street (CTV) 30.63
② CRAWLEY 30.49
Miles from London Bridge via Redhill
Controlled by Three Bridges (T) (ASC)
⑤ IFIELD 31.66
[SO 520] TBH 1 S : LBSC
Bewbush (UWC)(NT) 32.65
Kilnwood FP 33.45
⑤ FAYGATE 34.28
Roffey Road (10)(AHBC) 35.39
A264(T) 35.66
Brooks Lane FP (UWC)(NT) 35.23
④ LITTLEHAVEN (LH) 36.50
[SO 680] [SW 180] BTH 3 S : LBSC
Rusper Road (AHBC) 37.14
Parsonage Road
DOWN HORSHAM / UP HORSHAM
Horsham Jn 37.40 (Lon. Br.) 35.35 (W'loo)
(Engine Rd) Substation
Carriage Sdgs
DOWN SDG (MALTHOUSE)
Qy 38.08
UP LOOP
37.70 / 37.40 / 37.56
HORSHAM 37.56 (35.51 W'loo) (12)
UP SDG STH
DN SDG
former Signal Box 'listed'
Down Branch Sdgs 1,3,4
Down Branch Sdgs (12)
Bottom End Sdgs
Top End Sdgs
Field Sdgs
Engine Road
19C
19A

Other (UWC)(NT) on TBH 1
Itchingfield FP 40.66
Sharpenhurst No. 2 FP 41.28
Sharpenhurst No. 3 FP 41.39
Barns Green FP 42.01
Daux FP 44.54
Rats Bottom FP 47.23
Double FP 47.28
Wanseys FP 47.58
Frogs Hole FP 47.75
Windmill FP 48.04
Forty Steps FP 48.52
New Place FP 49.06

Panel C

19B
Miles from London Bridge via Redhill
(Itchingfield Jn) 40.54
40.33 (T) (BT)
② CHRIST'S HOSPITAL 40.07
40.66
A24(T) 39.59
⑦ Bakers (UWC) 39.55
Barns Green (AHBC) 42.18
Vale Wood (UWC) 42.45
Pratts Lower (UWC)(NT) 42.62
Rosier No. 2 (UWC) 44.35
Station Road 44.74
④ BILLINGSHURST 44.71
(T) (BT) 44.73
(BT) 44.51
[SO 520] TBH 1 S : LBSC
Hatfield No. 2 (UWC)(AHBC) 46.00
Adversane (AHBC) 46.31
Cray Lane (AHBC) 48.31
DOWN / UP
Hardham Vdct 50.66
⑨ PULBOROUGH 50.00
(PH) 49.74
R. Arun Vdct 50.11
Hardham Vdct 50.29-33
Thorndell Viaduct 52.74
Timberley Viaduct 53.36-44
(AY) 54.61
② AMBERLEY 54.62 ⑤
P
19D
20C : to Littlehampton
20C : to Worthing

Panel D

19C
Miles from London Bridge via Redhill
55.30-34 North Stoke Tunnel (83 yards)
South Stoke Viaduct
South Stoke South (UWC) 55.65
56.02
Pepperingeye (UWC) 56.30
Offham (UWC) 56.60
Black Rabbit (UWC)(NT) 57.03
(AR) 58.36
② ARUNDEL 58.28 (12)
[SO 520] TBH 1 S : LBSC
(LH) / (AR)
Vinnecombe (UWC)(NT)(AR) 60.64
Littlehampton Jn 60.57 (via Horsham) 19.25 (Brighton) 0.31 & Ford Jn
[SO 630] FJL 1 S : LBSC
Ford Bridge (River Arun)
Ford 0.00 19.36
[SO 520]
DN E CURVE / UP E CURVE
UP W C'VE / DN W C'VE
DOWN MAIN / UP MAIN
DOWN BRIGHTON 19.01 / UP BRIGHTON 19.75
DOWN HORSHAM / UP HORSHAM
UP SDG
UP LITTLEHTON
[SO 630] BLI 2 S : LBSC
[SO 520] TBH 2 S : LBSC
TBH 2 / TBH 1
DN MAIN 19.37 / UP MAIN 19.02
DN N CURVE (59.76)
60.25 / 60.31
COM 59.75 / 19.01 Arundel Jn N (to Bowerman's South) / Arundel Jn South
Hutchings (UWC) (19.03)
Triangle Controlled by Arundel (AR)

Arundel Junction area mileage trails
TBH 1 Miles from London Bridge via Redhill cease at Arundel Jn (N) and resume again at Littlehampton Jn on BLI 2 but measured via Ford Jn and reverse
BLI 1 Miles from Brighton run to Littlehampton Jn and over TBH 2 to Portsmouth Harbour
TBH 1 Miles from Ford Jn to Littlehampton Jn only
FJL 1 Miles from Ford Jn to Littlehampton Jn only
20C : to Ford & Chichester

Panel E

AMBERLEY CHALK PITS RAILWAY
(Southern Industrial History Centre Trust)

Main Strike Mine
Mixed 2' 0" & 3' 2½"gauge thus ......
Shed
Workshops
Workshop
LC'S (fool)
BROCKHAM
Woodyard Sdg
RR LC
AMBERLEY
CRAGSIDE
1435mm (4' 8½")

No signalling - "one engine in steam" or radio control
Not to scale. Amberley to Brockham is c500 yds
Gauge : 2 feet

www.amberleymuseum.co.uk   November 2008

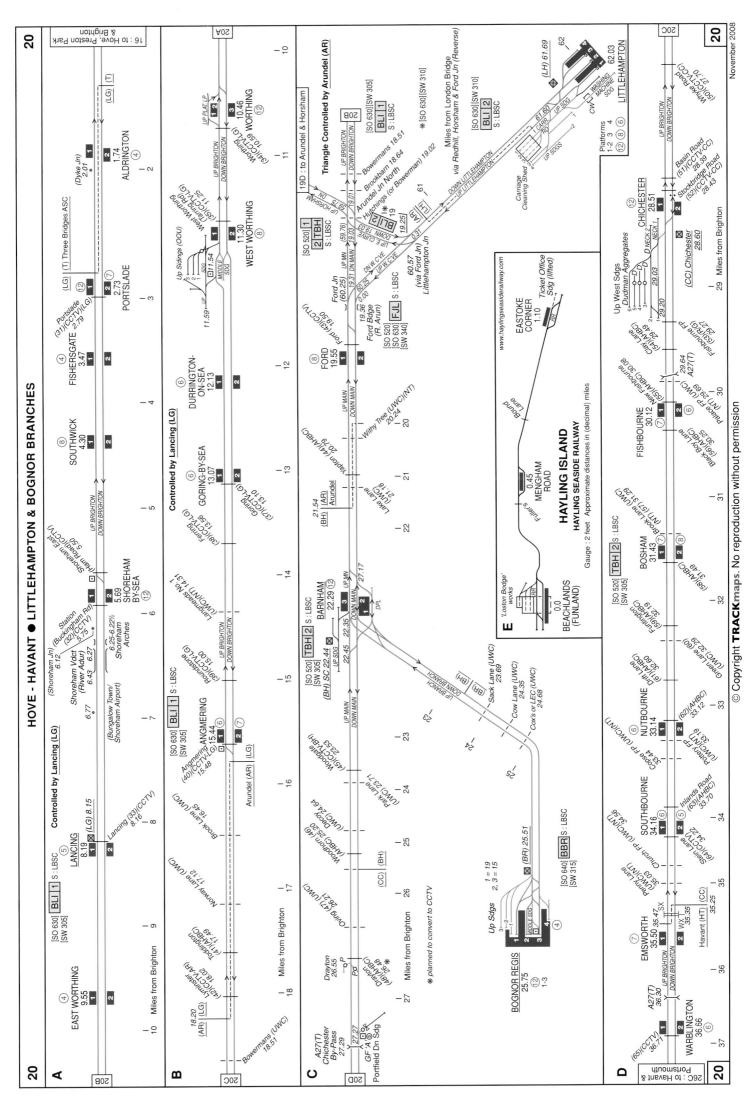

EARLSFIELD - WIMBLEDON - WEST BYFLEET ● NEW MALDEN - STRAWBERRY HILL - SHEPPERTON

A

WIMBLEDON TRAINCARE DEPOT (WD) · WPK

Wheel Lathe Shop

12 & 13 - Lifting Shop

Durnsford Road Sdgs · 6.04

Earlsfield Exit

Sections

2 : to Clapham Junction

R. Wandle · 5.72 · 5.63

EARLSFIELD · 5.46

[SW 105] BML 1 · S : LSW (London & Soton)

S : LSW

44A : to East Putney & Earl's Ct

Servicing Platform

Inspection shed · 'A' · 'B'

Wimbledon Stn Exit · 6.47

Wimbledon Park Sdgs · 6.28

6.15

6.26 · Durnsford Road

6.40

6.50

STAFF HALT

RUN ROUND No.2

ACCESS SDG No.2 · 6

ACCESS SDG No.1

Durnsford Rd Exit · 6.28

Flyover

TY = Wimbledon Top Yard

Shunt Panel

WIMBLEDON PARK · 7.50 · 53.59km

[SW 225] PPW · S : LSW

UP EAST PUTNEY · 7.54

DOWN EAST PUTNEY · 7.19 (W)oo via E. Putney)

Miles from Waterloo via East Putney

DISTRICT LINE

EASTBOUND

WESTBOUND

8.26

UP SDG 1 · UP SDG 2

CW

HAYDONS ROAD · 2.18

[SO 700] SMS 1

2

4 : to Tooting, Streatham & Tulse Hill

Controlled by Victoria Central (VC) ASC, at Clapham Jn (SMS Lines)

Platforms 1-4 PPW Buffer stops [55.15km (Ongar)]
[8.47 (W)oo via E. Putney)]
Platform 5-8 BML Centre 7.19 (W)oo via Earlsfield)
Platforms 9/10E SMS Centre & BS [3.05 (Streatham S. Jn)
[7.20 (Waterloo via Earlsfield)

(8.41) 55km

Platforms	
1 - 4	⑦
5 - 8	⑩
9	⑧
10	⑧

WIMBLEDON · 7.19 BML (70 ft)

1 2 3 4 5 6 7 8 9 E · COM

Bridge Ho. Umbrella

Wimbledon West (C) Jns · 7.30 7.27

Wimbledon East (A) Jns · 7.13

0.00 3.05 (7.22) (7.20)

MJW · 0.45km

Wimbledon (C) ASC

22 : to Sutton

47C : Tramlink to Croydon

1L : to Twickenham

[SO 700] SMS 2 · S : LSW

WIMBLEDON CHASE · 8.13 ⑧

[SW 105] BML 1 · S : LSW (London & Soton)

[SW 180] Raynes Park GF

RPE · S : LSW · Raynes Park GF · 9.04

RAYNES PARK · 8.51

8.48 · 8.34 · I SD

8.67 · 8.67

UP EPSOM · DN EPSOM

22 : to Chessington and Epsom

NEW MALDEN · 9.62

[SW 105] BML 1 · S : LSW (London & Soton)

UP SLOW · DOWN FAST · DOWN SLOW · UP FAST

A3 (Kingston Bypass) · 9.15

21B

Controlled by Wimbledon (W) ASC (BML & PPW Lines)

Miles from Waterloo via Earlsfield

Wimbledon North Jn

B

STRAWBERRY HILL DEPOT · i/c Siemens

[SW 245] SHF · S : LSW

Strawberry Hill Jn 12.28

[SW 245] TSJ · S : LSW

(CCTV-F) 12.26

UP STRAWBERRY HILL · DOWN STRAWBERRY HILL

Strawberry Hill Jn · 12.22

No.1 SIDING

12.53 · 12.45

No.5 SDG

UP SHEPPERTON SPUR · DOWN SHEPPERTON SPUR

Staff crossing 12.33

Staff crossing

Field · FULWELL REC

FULWELL · 12.75

Fulwell Jn · 12.56 · 14.53

2 NMS 1 · [SW 190] · S : LSW

Miles from Waterloo via Twickenham

Fulwell Tunnels (Wellington Rd) (62 yds) · 13.03-06

UP SHEPPERTON · DOWN SHEPPERTON

Percy Rd (CCTV-F) 14.51

HAMPTON · 14.47

1 2

PERCY · 14.51

Controlled by Feltham (F) ASC

HAMPTON WICK · 12.44

DOWN KINGSTON · UP KINGSTON

TEDDINGTON · 13.54

COM · 12.53

14.29 · Shacklegate Jn

Commissioning Shed (Siemens) · 14.35

Carriage Shed (Siemens)

'A' = Carriage Shed
'B' = Commissioning Shed (Siemens)

SD

HAMPTON COURT · 14.76

UP HAMPTON CT · DOWN HAMPTON CT · 14.32

2 RD · Summer Road (CCTV-WK) 14.51

THAMES DITTON · 14.01

Ember River Bridge · 14.68

[SW 195] HAM · S : LSW

Kingston Bridge (River Thames)

KINGSTON · 12.09 · 12.34

⑧ (W) Wimbledon

(F) Feltham · [SW 190] NMS 1 · S : LSW

NORBITON · 11.24

⑧ (W) Wimbledon

DOWN BAY

12.0

Malden (Elm Lane) (OCTW)

(W)

Woking (WK)

Berrylands Jn · 11.19

BERRYLANDS · 10.78

12

NEW MALDEN · 9.68 · 9.62

[SW 105] BML 1 · S : LSW (L & Soton)

10.19 · 10.18

9.71 · 9.77

10.16

SURBITON · 12.03

3 4

12.40 · 12.23

[SW 105] BML 1 · S : LSW (L & Soton)

5A : Model Railway

HAM · [SW 195]

UP SLOW · UP FAST · DOWN FAST · DOWN SLOW

Hampton Court Jn · 13.27

13.22 · 13.05

13.40 · 13.34 · 13.63

vdct-arches FA41-FA1 · 13.22 · 13.33

Up Sdg

[SW 200] NGL · S : LSW

HINCHLEY WOOD · 14.04

[SW 195] BML 1 · S : LSW (L & Ston)

ESHER · 14.31

HERSHAM · 15.73

WALTON-ON-THAMES · 17.06

UP SLOW · UP FAST · DOWN FAST · DOWN SLOW

[SW 190] NMS 2 · S : LSW

UPPER HALLIFORD · 17.34

SUNBURY · 16.64

KEMPTON PARK · 16.28

P

25A : to Virginia Water

19.74 Addlestone Jn

[SW 255] VWW · S : LSW

WEYBRIDGE · 19.22

Weybridge Jn · 19.33

GSP

DN CHERTSEY · UP CHERTSEY

River Wey · 19.54-52

River Wey Viaduct · 19.08

22 : to Efingham Junction

DN COBHAM · UP COBHAM

Controlled by Woking (WK) ASC

23 : to Woking

SHEPPERTON · 18.73

Miles from Waterloo via Twickenham

Servicing Platform · 18.25

UP SDG · DOWN SDG · 18.65

WEST BYFLEET · 21.54

[SW 255] AJB · S : LSW

M25 · Byfleet · 20.53

BYFLEET & NEW HAW · 20.27

20.56 20.27 · 20.32

20.00 · 20.18 · 20.47

BYFLEET LOOP · -0.02 · 0.20 · 0.25 · 0.67

Wey Navigation Canal · 20.56

Miles from Waterloo

Controlled by Wimbledon (W) ASC

© Copyright **TRACKmaps**. No reproduction without permission

November 2008

WIMBLEDON - EFFINGHAM JN./WEST CROYDON - BOXHILL AND ASSOCIATED LINES

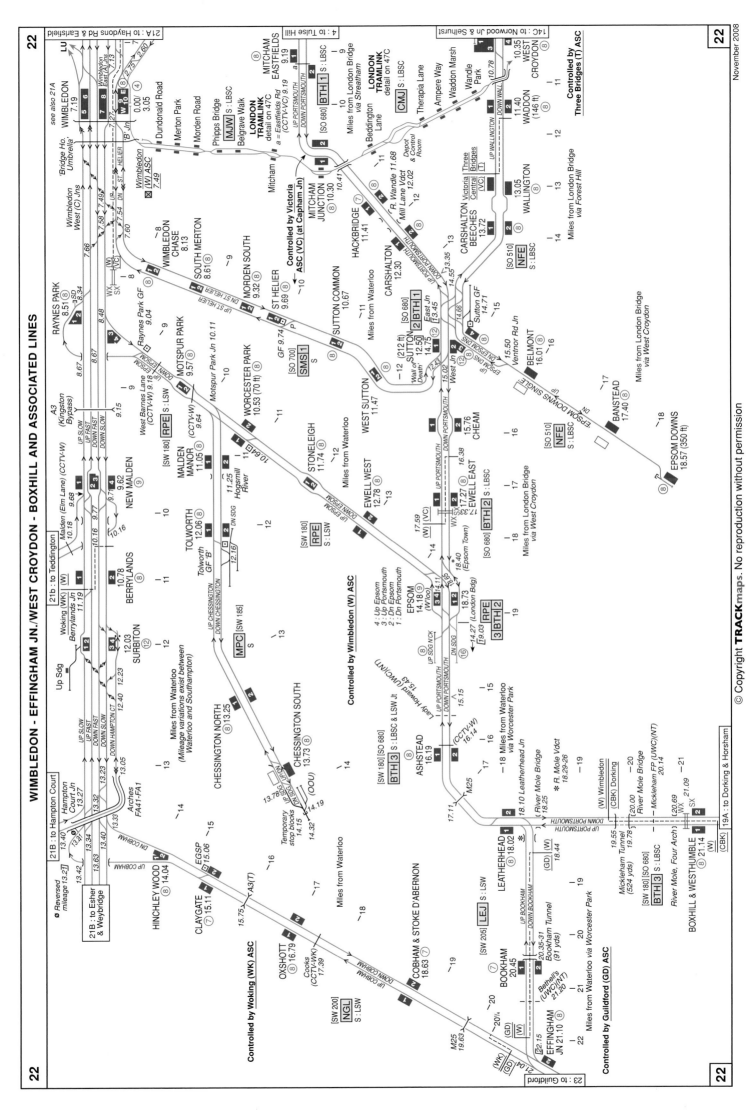

WEST BYFLEET - WOKING - GUILDFORD ● EFFINGHAM JN - GUILDFORD - ASH

21B : to Weybridge & Surbiton

22 : to Surbiton

22 : to Leatherhead

WEST BYFLEET 21.54
⑫ 1
BML 1 S : LSW (London & Southampton)
[SW 105]

EFFINGHAM JUNCTION 21.10
⑧ 1 21.04
2 22.15
21.25
21.38
DN SDG 21.27 21.13
Amec Rail Plant

HORSLEY 22.12
⑧ 1
2

Platforms
1-4 ⑫
5 ⑫ Up ⑭ Down
6 ⑥

[SW 105] BML 1 S : LSW
Former Signal Box 'listed'
* Mileage calculation excludes new Up Bay Platform 3

25.65
24.00
23.70
East End Sdg
24.06
24.00
(WK) ASC 24.20

WOKING 24.27 *
1
3
4
5
6
24.14
24.18
#

[SW 200] NGL S : LSW

GSP 25.20
☒ 1 2

CLANDON 25.26
⑦ 1 2

Merrow 26.61

HURDLES RD
SHORT BLOCK
PEN RD
No.2 UP SDG
No.1 REC
6 DEAD
5 DEAD
4 DEAD
3 END
MIDDLE BLOCK
24.40
TOP SHED
BOTTOM SHED
BOTTOM / KNYBER
CROOK
No.1 BDG
CABIN
24.62
24.56
Woking Jn
24.30
Day Aggregates
Redland Aggregates
★ Balfour Beatty
Woking Down Yard
WKG 8

Woking Up Yard
WKG 9
8
7
2
1
5
4
25.03 3
24.77
25.12
25.05

Qy
RECEPTION
No.2 RECEPTION
No.1 RECEPTION
DOWN GUILDFORD
UP GUILDFORD
25.00

25
26
27

WORPLESDON 26.65
⑫ 2 1
(WK) 26.05
(GD)

LONDON ROAD (Guildford) 28.47
⑧ 2 1

London Road Vdct

UP COBHAM
DOWN COBHAM
Miles from Waterloo via Cobham

29.23
29.26
29.60
30 (via Woking)
Guildford New Line Jn
29.50 Guildford North Jn

GTW1 WPH1 NGL
(a) ASH 30.05
(b) COBHAM 30.07
(c) MAIN 30.14
30.35
30.27 (via Woking; mileage reversal at 30.20 to GTW)
29.52
29.59

* 30.20 [Woking end
[Platforms 3-8
COBHAM BAY
29.68

GUILDFORD
a a a
a3
c
b b
UP ASH
DN ASH
a4 b
a5 a6 b b
a7 a8 b
UP MAIN
DN MAIN
UM
DM
(GD) ASC 30.40
☒ 30.43
Chalk Tunnel (845 yds)

Platforms 2-8 designated
London End
Portsmouth End/South End
Platforms 1,2,3,4,5,6,8 a (not 7)
Lines reversible except Platforms 2 & 4
(a) ASH (b) COBHAM

24A & 26A : to Haslemere, Dorking & Redhill

Controlled by Guildford (GD) ASC

PERTURBATION SDG or NORTH BOX SDG
30.02
29.77

Carriage Sdgs
3 2 1
TRIMLEY
SDG
DOCK SIG
Dock
UP ASH SDG

A3 31.20
UP ASH
DOWN ASH

[SO 560] [SW 110] WPH1 S : LSW

Platforms
1 ⑧
2 ⑧ Up ⑫ Down
3-7 ⑫
8 ⑩

WANBOROUGH 34.29
④ 1 2

Miles from Waterloo
via Worplesdon & Guildford (reverse)
at 30.20 (WPH 1)

KNAPHILL
● WOKING MINIATURE RAILWAY
(see inset below)
[SW 105] BML 1 S : LSW (London & Southampton)
Controlled by Woking (WK) ASC
UP SLOW
UP FAST
DOWN FAST
DOWN SLOW

Miles from Waterloo
(Mileage variations exist between
Waterloo and Southampton/Exeter)

WOKING MINIATURE RAILWAY SOCIETY LTD
7¼" gauge   1200 metres
www.mizensrailway.co.uk

SANTA'S HALT
TWITCHEN MANOR
BONSEY LANE
(alighting platform)
Carriage Shed
Station Building
Loco Shed
Pit
N
A

BROOKWOOD 27.79
⑫ 1
28.12
2
EGSP
27.63

Pirbright Jn (29.39 mean)
29.31
29½
29.60
29.49
30

[SW 120] PAA 1 S : LSW

UP ALTON
DOWN ALTON
24C : to Farnborough
24C : to Aldershot

[SW 120] NSA S : LSW
[SW 120] [SW 265]
UP BRANCH
DN BRANCH
0.00

24C : to Aldershot
24C : to North Camp

ASH 49.18
⑧ 1
④ 2 48.15
(CCT/4/GD)
49
(former Ash Jn) **COM**
48.34 35.50
S : SE S : LSW
[SW 265]
2 GTW 1

UP BLACKWATER
DN BLACKWATER

Aldershot South Jn 50.01
[SW 265] GTW 2 S : SE

Miles from Charing Cross via Redhill

November 2008
© Copyright **TRACKmaps**. No reproduction without permission

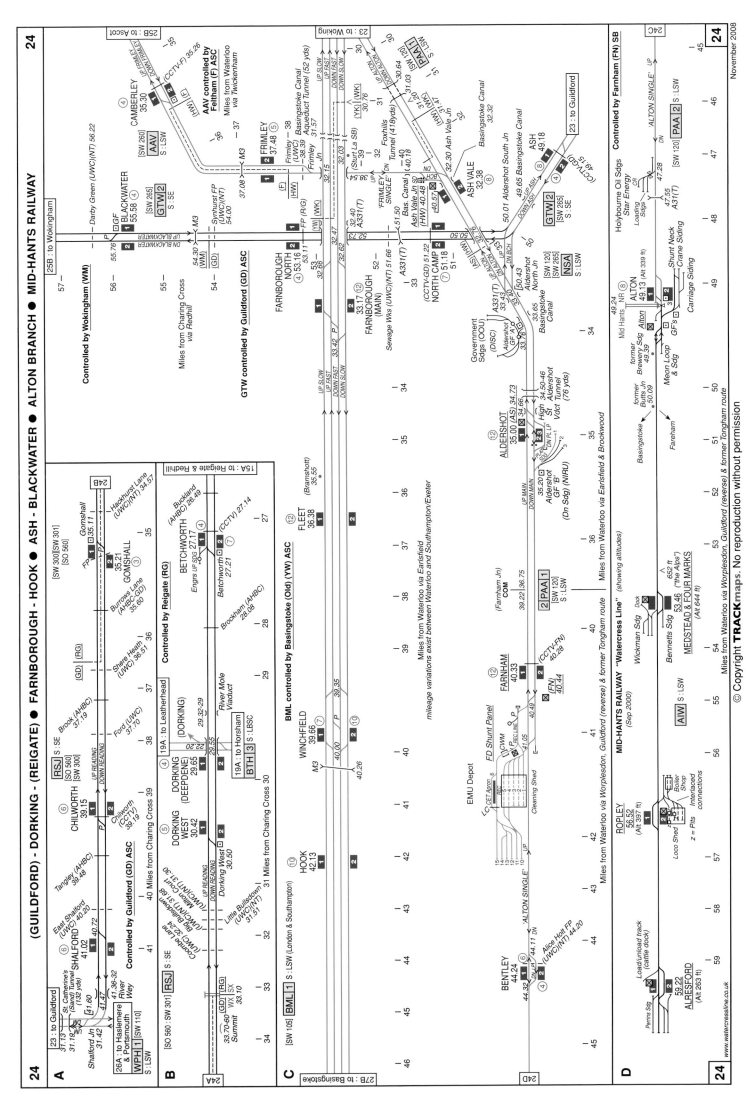

FELTHAM - READING ● WINDSOR BRANCH ● CHERTSEY BRANCH

A

Black Potts Vdct (CCTV) 23.69
(R. Thames) 24.74 24.63

WINDSOR & ETON
RIVERSIDE
25.48
[SW 210] RDG 1 S : LSW
1 2
GF 25.40

(10) 25.23 (9)

DATCHET
23.63
(8)
1 2
Mays (CCTV) 23.74

Controlled by Feltham (F) ASC

LONGCROSS
25.11
(8)
1 2

SUNNINGDALE
26.71
(8)
1 2
London Road (CCTV) 26.66

SUNNYMEADS
22.48
(8)
1 2

WRAYSBURY
21.40
[SW 250] SWE S:LSW
1 2

20.40 M25 Bridges

19.59 Wraysbury River

EGHAM
(CCTV) 21.08
(8)
1 2
21.02

Pooley Green (CCTV) 20.51
Trotsworth Lane (CCTV) 19.81

OOU
Former Oil Depot

SWX

Rusham (AHBC) 21.61
Stroude (UWC) 22.51

VIRGINIA
WATER
23.15
(8)
1 2
23.06

23.01
(8) 2
(8) 1 24.74
(7) 24.65
(8) 24.71

24.24
24.20

Lyne Bridge (M25)
(Rail suspension bridge)

23.37

Miles from Waterloo
via Weybridge

Chertsey 22.32
CHERTSEY
22.25 (5)
VWW S:LSW
(CCTV) 22.20
(F) 1
2

ADDLESTONE
20.71 (8)
[SW 255]
20.06 River Wey
20.65
(CCTV+WK)
(F) 1
2
Woking (WK)
19.74 Addlestone Jn

-0.02
21B : to Weybridge
21B : to Woking

AJB
[SW 255]

Up Windsor
Down Windsor

Up Main
Down Main

Up Chertsey
Down Chertsey

ASHFORD (Middx)
17.40
(8)
1 2

Oakmead (UWC) 18.30

East Yard
EMU Berthing Sdgs
4 3 2 1

Shortwood
Common Crossing
(UWC)(NT) 18.44

Staines
Staines 19.52
West Jn 19.48
Staines East Jn
19.39 19.32
EAST SDG

Staines Bridge
(R. Thames) 19.40
STAINES
19.02
19.26
[SW 210] RDG 1 S : LSW
(8)

FELTHAM
14.68
(8)
1 2
Grid Sdg
GF 'A' 14.65 (F) ASC 14.60

Feltham West
(Bedfont La.) (CCTV) 14.74

DOWN MAIN
UP MAIN

Feltham
13.35
14.38
[SW 210] RDG 1 S : LSW

Hounslow Jn
14.09
[SW 230] HOU S:LSW
14.39
HJW
13.03
Whitton
Jn

[SW 210] S:LSW

1L : to Richmond & Waterloo

1L : to Willesden & Waterloo

25B

B

ASCOT
28.79
[SW 210] RDG 1 S : LSW
1 2 28.66
29.04
29.18
29.28
3
No.5 SDG
M & EE SDG
DN PL LP

Controlled by Feltham (F) ASC

Miles from Waterloo
via Twickenham

25A

Englemere (UWC) 29.36
• (Ascot West) 30.03

UP MAIN
DOWN MAIN

BAGSHOT
32.08
[SW 260]
AAV S:LSW
(4)
1
33.60
33.66
Jenkins Hill (UWC) 33.23
Bagshot Tunnel (121 yds)

Guildford Road Viaduct

UP FRIMLEY
DOWN FRIMLEY

24C : to Camberley

MARTIN'S HERON
31.09
(8)
1 2
(WM) 31.20

BRACKNELL
32.24
(8)
1 2
(WM)

34.07
A329(M)
Waterloo (AHBC) 34.76
34.34 (WM)
Star Lane (CCTV) 35.30
Smiths (UWC) 35.73

[SW 210] RDG 1 S : LSW

Miles from Waterloo via Twickenham

CROWTHORNE
58.66
[SW 265] GTW 2 S : SE
Controlled by Wokingham (WM)
(4)
1 2

Harvey's (UWC)(NT) 58.12

SANDHURST
57.22
(3)
1 2

24C : to Blackwater

WOKINGHAM
62.08
(8)
1 2
Wokingham Jn
COM 61.72
61.59
36.35
(WM)
DN GDS LP

UP MAIN
DOWN MAIN

WINNERSH
TRIANGLE
64.72
(8)
1 2
(WM)

WINNERSH
64.10
(8)
1 2
63.42
M4
64.04 (R) (WM)

EARLEY
66.01
(8)
1 2
65.70
65.61 (R)
65.16
River Loddon
66.04 (R) (WM)

Miles from Charing Cross via Redhill

RNJ [SW 210] S SE
68.00 (R)
67.77
67.76
Reading Spur Jn
[SW 210] RDG 2 S : SE

3 : 3A :
to Ealing Broadway
and Paddington

[GW 103] MLN 1 GW
Reading New Jn
35.40
UP RELIEF
DOWN RELIEF
UP MAIN
DOWN MAIN
UP RDG SPUR
DN RDG SPUR
UP SOUTHERN
DN SOUTHERN
68.39
68.32
68.34
68.48
EMU sdgs
W
WX
D

27A : to Reading

Controlled by
Reading (R) ASC

Miles from Waterloo via Twickenham

Controlled by Feltham (F) ASC

A

Controlled by Guildford (GD) ASC

23 : to Guildford

St Catherine's (Sand) Tunnel (132 yds)
Chalk Tunnel (845 yds)
DN MAIN 31.13 31.01 UM
DN MAIN 31.19 31.01
Shalford Jn 31.42

RSJ
41.60↑ 41.47 41.36 41.32
R. Wey
UP RDG
DN RDG
24A : to Shalford, Dorking & Redhill

UP MAIN
DOWN MAIN
Miles from Waterloo via Woking

Farncombe East (MCB) CCTV/WZ 33.29
[WZ] (12) 1
FARNCOMBE 33.38 33.47
Farncombe West (MCB) 33.53 33.54
(10)

(AHBC) 36.26
GODALMING 34.37 (12)
[WZ] 2 1
MILFORD 36.21 (8)(7)
2 1 [WZ]
(EW)

WITLEY 38.36 (8)
2 1

[SW 110] WPH 1 S : LSW

UP PLAT LOOP
UP SDG 1 UP SDG 3
42.65 42.50
43.13
HASLEMERE 42.79 (12)
[EW] 2

Hammer Lane (UWC)(NT) 44.41
(UWC)(NT)

B

26A

LIPHOOK 46.67 (8)
1
2 (EW)
47.15 (PF)

(EW) 50.10
Liss Forest FP (UWC)(NT) 50.49
Liss Common (AHBC) 50.75
(CCTV) 51.40
LISS 51.35 (8)
1
2 (PF)

Princes Bridge (AHBC) 52.12
Stodham FP (UWC)(NT) 52.60
Sheet (AHBC) 53.72
Kings Ramsden (AHBC) 54.10

PETERSFIELD 54.71 (12)
54.65 (PF)
1 (HT)
GF
2 (PF)
55.00

56.42 (A3)
57.05 (PF)
Buriton FP (UWC)(NT) 57.27
Buriton Tunnel (485 yds)
57.46 57.68 57.46
58.10

(Woodcroft Halt) 59.72
Didworth (UWC)(NT) 59.43

[SW 110] WPH 1 S : LSW
Idsworth (UWC)(NT) 61.14

ROWLANDS CASTLE 63.18 (6)
1
2

Fareham Tunnel No. 1 (147 yards)
Fareham Tunnel No. 2 (553 yards)
83.12 83.20 83.21

On the Knowle Single Line between 79.14 and 83.58
4th Rail installed but no running contact

[ETF]
Controlled by Eastleigh (E) ASC
28B : to Botley & Eastleigh

C

26B
65 : to Chichester
20D : to Chichester

DOWN MAIN
DOWN BTON
UP BTON
UP MAIN

Havant Jn
37.25
* Havant New Lane (66) (CCTV)(HT) 37.26
37.32

Havant (HT) ASC
37.28/66.20
[SW 110] WPH 1 [SW 110]
2 TBH 2 [SO 520]
HAVANT 37.41 (12)
S : LSW 1 | 2
S : LBSC
Havant East 37.57

[SW 110] [SO 520]
WPH 2 (6)
BEDHAMPTON 38.14
Havant West 37.57
1
Bedhampton (69)(CCTV)(HT) 38.10

A3(M) 39.00
Farlington Jn 40.33
40.38 40.41
Portcreek Viaduct 41.03-06

[SW 140] FJJ S : LBSC
91.14
91.09
DN SPUR 91.02
UP SPUR 91.02

[SW 140] SDP 2
COSHAM Cosham Jn 90.06 90.43
1 41.04
2
Cosham 36.01 (CCTV)(HT)
S : LBSC/LSW Jt

★ A27(T) 90.79-41.00
41.03 Portcreek Jn

HILSEA 41.41 (8)
1
2
[SW 110] [SO 520] WPH 2 S : LBSC/LSW

88.37
88.14
M27
PORTCHESTER 87.35 (5)
1
2 SDP 2
[SW 140]

87 Miles from Waterloo via Eastleigh
Priddys Hard
Tichborne Way
Forest Way
former Bedenham Sdgs OOU
87.21
86.78 [HT] FTB S : LSW
86.10

Quay Viaduct 84.77 85.04
Wallington Viaduct 85.32-43
Eastleigh ASC (E) 84.68
'GOSPORT SINGLE' CLOSED
Newgate Lane (AOCL) 85.08

Platforms
3 (8)
2 (7)
1 (9)
Hanson
DN SDG 1
DN SDG 2
Fareham 'A' 84.21 D
Fareham 'B' 84.25
Fareham West Jn (South) 84.27
FAREHAM 84.21 (12)
1 2 SDP 2 [SW 140]
Fareham East Jn (North) 84.09
1 SDP 1 S : LSW
[SW 140]

[SW 135] ETF S : LSW
Fareham North Jn 83.57
83.46
A27 (M27) Link 11.40
DOWN NETLEY
UP NETLEY 11.16

SWANWICK 10.50 (7)
1
2
Hamble River Viaduct (Bridge 29)
29 : to St. Denys & Southampton

Miles from former Southampton Terminus

KNOWLE SINGLE 83.12
DN UP

All lines between Fareham (excl) and Southbourne (excl)
also Portsmouth Harbour and Petersfield (excl)
controlled by Havant (HT) ASC

FRATTON TRAINCARE DEPOT (FR)
Inspection & Carriage Cleaning Shed

Old Yard (No. 2 - fuel tanks)
43.26 43.35
Fratton East 43.41
DOWN MAIN 43.33
UP MAIN
Fratton 43.46
43.64
FRATTON 43.46
1 2 3
WPH 2 [SW 110] [SO 520]
S : LBSC/LSW
43.70 43.75
Fratton West 44
Fratton Depot GF 43.67 (12)
CW SOUTHSEA
CATTLE DOCK SDG
WASH

Blackfriars Jn 44.29
Down Carriage Sdgs 44.24
PORTSMOUTH & SOUTHSEA
44.47 (Low Level)
4 a PAS (10)
b 3 a
2
1
44.50
44.50-45 Station Viaduct 44.45
(High Level)
UP MAIN
DOWN MAIN
DOWN & UP FRATTON
BACK ROAD
44.39

45.14
45.22
45.36
PORTSMOUTH HARBOUR
1 (8)
3
4
5 (12)
Pier and arches

[SW 110] [SO 520] WPH 2 S : LBSC/LSW Jt

Miles from Brighton
37 38 39 40 41 42 43 44 45

November 2008

© Copyright TRACKmaps. No reproduction without permission

READING - BASINGSTOKE - WINCHESTER - SHAWFORD

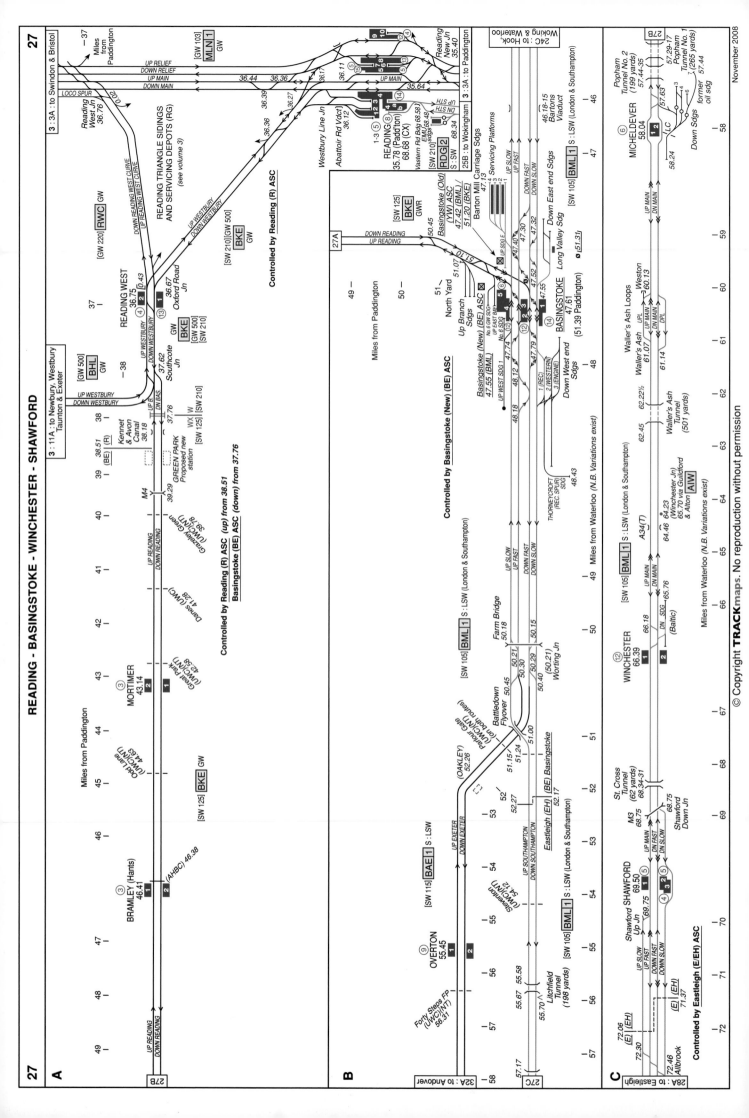

November 2008

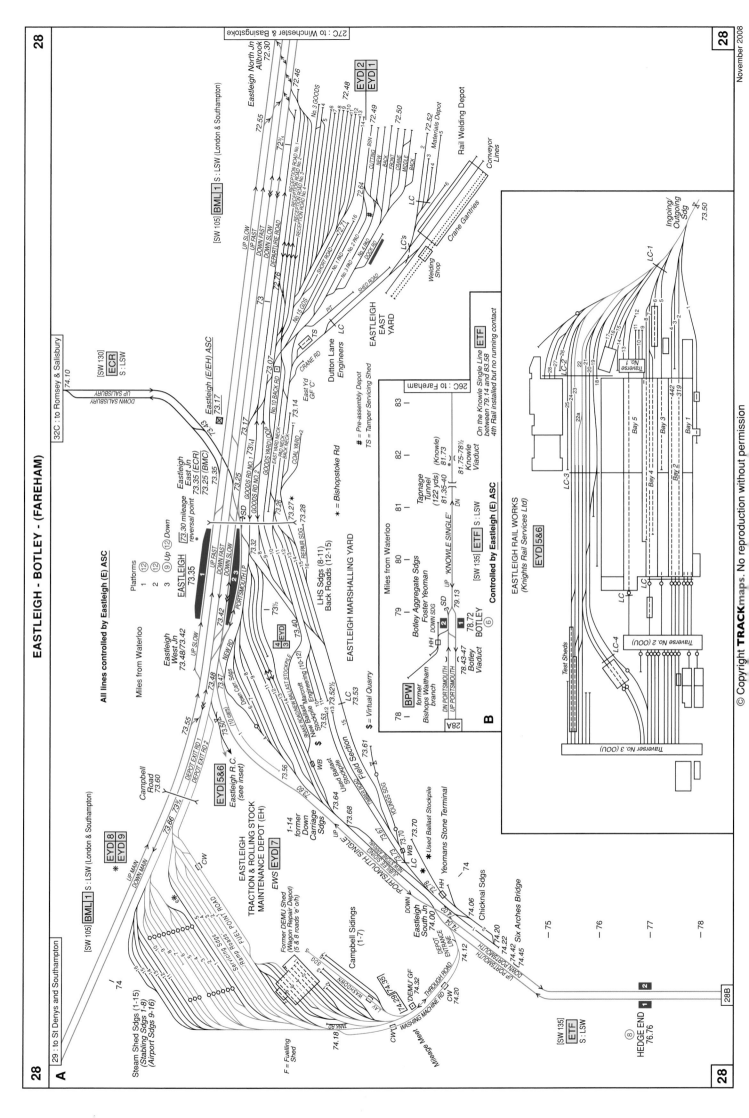

EASTLEIGH - BOTLEY - (FAREHAM)

SOUTHAMPTON

A

www.steamtrain.co.uk

MONKS BROOK HALT

LC

Lakeside Tunnel

Lakes

LC

EASTLEIGH LAKESIDE RAILWAY
Dual 7¼" & 10½" gauge   2100 yards

Loading Ramp

Workshop Traverser

7¼" only

EASTLEIGH PARKWAY   1 2 3

LC

—74

—75

—76

—77

Miles from Eastleigh

Miles from Waterloo

Miniature railway • see left

[28A : to Eastleigh]

[SW 105] BML 1 S : LSW (London & Soton)

SOUTHAMPTON AIRPORT ⑫ (PARKWAY) 74.66   1   2

Swaythling (UWC)(NT) 75.26   M27 75.08

SWAYTHLING ④ 75.56   1   2

ST. DENYS ① 77.10   1   2   3   4 1.59

Plat 2 ⑥   Plats 1,3,4 ⑦

St. Denys Jn   77.15

Adelaide Road (CCTV) 1.69

Itchen River Bridge (2) 2.17-23

BITTERNE 2.36 ⑥   1   2

SHOLING 4.58 ⑧   1

WOOLSTON 4.11 ⑦   1   2 GF 4.21

CET Discharge

NETLEY 6.45 ⑧   1   2 GF 'B' 6.42

HAMBLE 7.19 ④   1   2 Hamble GF (OOU) 7.10

OOU Hamble Rd (open/booms)   Hamble Rd (open)
former BP Oil Ltd

BURSLEDON 8.49 ⑧   1   2

[26C : to Fareham]

Miles from former Southampton Terminus

DOWN NETLEY   UP NETLEY

[SW 140] SDP 1 S : LSW

Miniature railway see below

77.68 COM (Northam Short Mile)

NORTHAM TRAINCARE FACILITY
SW Trains/Siemens Transportation Systems Ltd (STSL)
Shed 213m (10 x 20m or 9 x 23m coaches) - OTS = overhead
traction supply: Track 4 - bogie drop pit
WL - Wheel Lathe   BL - Battery loco

All lines controlled by Eastleigh (E) ASC

78.17 Northam Rd Bridge   78.20 (Northam)

UP FAST DOWN FAST UP SLOW DOWN SLOW UP MAIN DOWN MAIN

Mount Pleasant (CCTV) 77.54

77.68 # 78.00

Northam Jn (78.15)   78.52

Southampton Tunnel (528 yds)

4th rail elec

UM 78.28½-18   DM 78.28½-17

SOUTHAMPTON CENTRAL ⑬ 79.19   b 1 a   b 3 a   b 4 a ⑥

79.37 79.55 79.68 79.78

UP GOODS LOOP UP FAST UP SLOW DOWN SLOW DOWN FAST DN LOOP DN DP EXT

[SW 105] BML 2 S : LSW (Southampton & Dorchester)

Miles from Waterloo (NB variations exist)

Berkeley Jn

Mountbatten Way

MILLBROOK ⑧ 80.11   1   2

MILLBROOK FREIGHTLINER TERMINAL

Crane area

Church Lane 80.27 80.32

West Bay Road

NR ABP (TMO) ARR DEP

UP MAIN 80.52 DOWN MAIN 80.45 80.70

[30A : to Redbridge]

MIS Ansa Logistics Terminal CR ENGINE RD BULK RD

Mdk Dk Ent/Exit No. 12 Gate

SOUTHAMPTON WESTERN DOCKS (104-101 Berths)

Mayflower Cruise Terminal LC P & O

Concrete apron

105 shed 105 Berth 106 Berth 107 Berth 107 shed

Container handling area

Gypsum Stone loading pad 108 handling area 108 Berth 109 Berth WB

River Test

Town Quay

Associated British Ports

Berth

79   79.00 79.04 Canute Rd 79.20

[SW 145] SOY S : LSW (London & Southampton)

Southampton Terminus

EASTERN DOCKS SINGLE   UP 78.17   DN

Central Road (TMO)

NR ABP No. 3 Rail Gate Maritime Way 41 Berth Shed

Queen Elizabeth II Terminal (38/39 berth)

Ocean Dock

78.52 Chapel Road (AOCL)

SOUTHAMPTON EASTERN DOCKS

Empress Dock

River Itchen

78.37 78.43

NORTHAM ARRDEP 78.24 (STSL) WASHER SHUNTING NECK

Sea Wall Main Traincare Facility (OTS)

Servicing platforms

77.25/1.45 77.30 77.44 No.1 REC No.2 REC SHED NK CW WM

No.2 NECK No.1 REC 77.58 78.01

77.03 1.54

former Southampton Up Yard (Bevois Park Sidings)

BML 1 BML 2 78.76

DN SDG EAST BAY SDG DN SDG WEST

B

ROYAL VICTORIA RAILWAY, Netley
10¼" gauge
About 2½ miles of track gauge

Carriage Shed Loading Spur Pit Loco Sheds

LC PICCADILLY   LC CHAPEL ROAD

A - B Trackbed of former standard gauge Hospital branch from Netley, closed '55

www.royalvictoriarailway.co.uk

November 2008

© Copyright TRACKmaps. No reproduction without permission

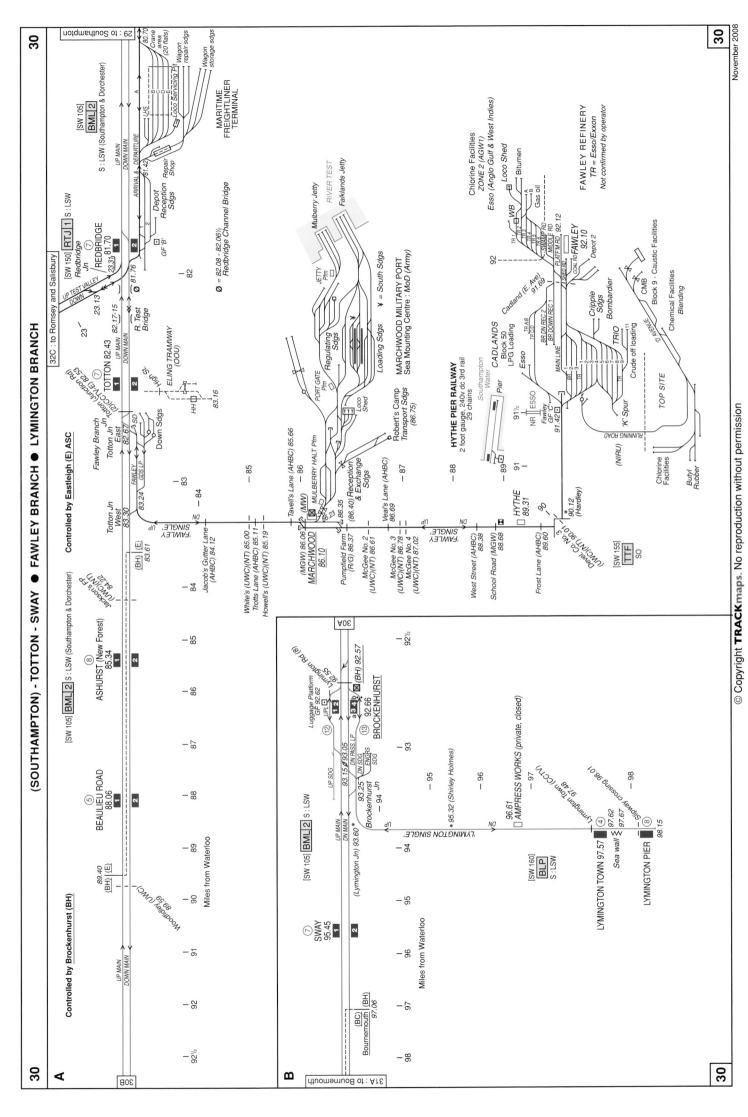

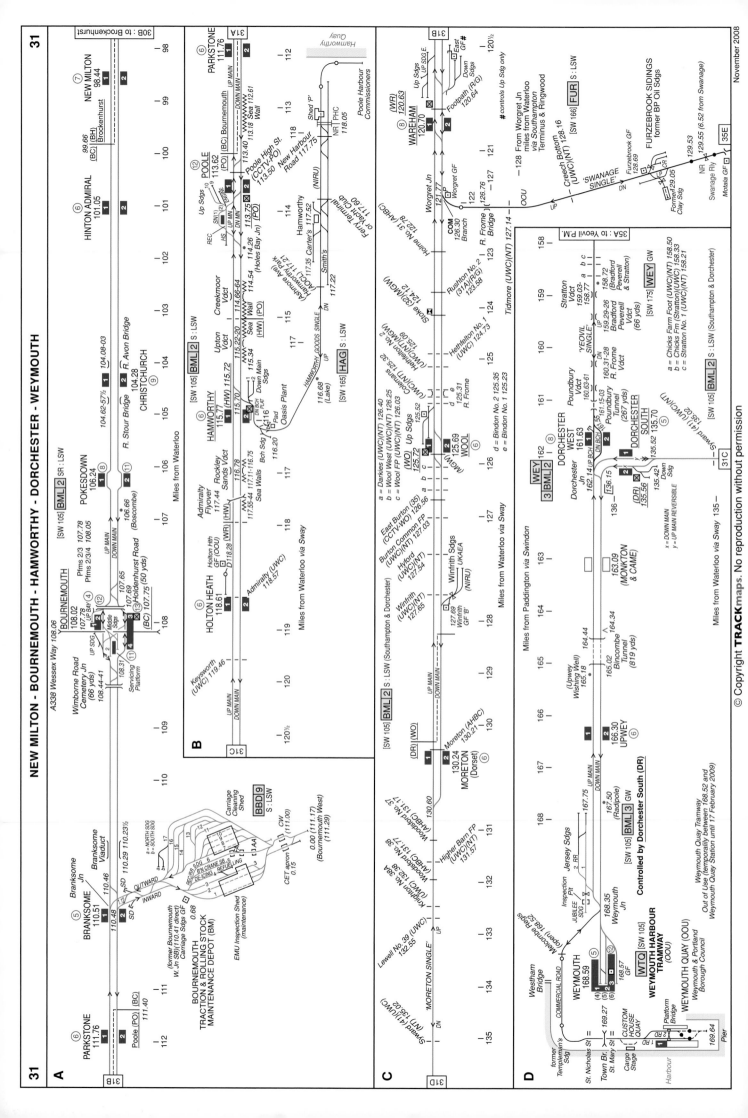

NEW MILTON - BOURNEMOUTH - HAMWORTHY - DORCHESTER - WEYMOUTH

© Copyright TRACKmaps. No reproduction without permission

November 2008

WHITCHURCH - SALISBURY ● LUDGERSHALL BRANCH ● SALISBURY - ROMSEY - EASTLEIGH and REDBRIDGE

A

27B : to Basingstoke

WHITCHURCH (Hants) 59.08
A34(T)
59.36

[SW 115] BAE 1 S : LSW

Hurstbourne Viaduct
61.18-11

62.47

Controlled by Basingstoke (BE) ASC

UP EXETER
DOWN EXETER

Enham (UWC)(NT) 64.35

ANDOVER 66.19
Andover GF 66.27

Up Yard

66.54

BRANCH
DN 1
A303(T) 67.16

Gallachers (UWC)(NT) 66.75

A303(T) (Red Post Jn)
LUD 1 67.61

Weyhill 1.71
Monxton Viaduct or Phil Hill Brook 68.42-38

1.52 A303(T)
0.00 (LUDGERSHALL)
5.64
5.71 WD/NR Ludgershall Jn
5.61 (LUDGERSHALL)

[SW 115] LUD 2 M & SW Jn

Ludgershall Jn

6.08 6 Pfm
Dock
Horse Sdgs

6.15 Perham Jn

Canopy
LC

Shed
Shed
CY

LUDGERSHALL
Ministry of Defence (Army)

GRATELEY 72.49
(SY) (BE) Basingstoke
72.57
73.20

Miles from Waterloo

B

32A

[SW 115] BAE 1 S : LSW

(Idmiston) 77.38

78.00 (BE)
78.07 (Porton)
(SY)

Targetts (UWC)(NT) 78.21

Laverstock North Jn 82.05
82.11
UP 82
LAVERSTOCK LOOP [SW 115 & 150]
82.57 82.37
Laverstock South Jn 95.61
96.05

LAV BR (LSW)

UP MAIN
DOWN MAIN
UP DEAN
DN DEAN

Sir Frederick's Bridge or Milford Clarendon Park Curve

92.05 (Alderbury Jn)
92.75
93.67

Salisbury Tunnel Jn 82.36

Fisherton Tunnel (445 yds)
A36(T) 82.63
83.00

East Carriage Holding Sdgs
(NIRU)

83.38 (SY)
83.43

SALISBURY

Platforms
2&3
4
6

UP 83.28
REC LINE 1
UP MAIN
DN SDG 1
DN SDG 2
ARR/DEP
THRO SDG

Salisbury East Sdgs

Berthing Sdgs

Maintenance Shed

SALISBURY TRAINCARE DEPOT (SA)

CET
DEPOT REC
PLATFORM
DOWN MAIN
W (S) RAILWAY
ENGRS

DEP
SDG
CW1
CW2
H

83.63

84.00 83.72
COM

Gramshaw Rd (UWC)(NT) 84.22

'Fisherton Short Mile'

2 BAE 1

[SW 170] SAL GW

Quidhampton (Tinkerpit) Broadlands Quarry Imerys Minerals Ltd

132.54

84.35
84.36 A36(T) (Skew Bridge)

85.14
85.37 Wilton Jn

Miles from Paddington via Swindon

(WILTON) 132
Wilton Sth Jn 132
GF 132.25
Wilton 86.11
86.18 A36(T)
86.25

[SW 115] BAE 2 S : LSW (Salisbury & Yeovil)

33A : to Westbury

33B : to Tisbury & Yeovil Jn

UP WESTBURY
DN WESTBURY

UP EXETER
DOWN EXETER

Miles from Waterloo via Andover

Controlled by Salisbury (SY)

East Grimstead 90.10

West Grimstead (UWC)(NT) 90.64

(OOU)

East Grimstead

[SW 150] RTJ 2 S : LSW

Miles from Waterloo via Andover

32C

C

Eastleigh (E/EH) ASC 73.17

BML 1
Eastleigh East Jn 73.25

28A : to Basingstoke
73.35

28A : to Eastleigh

UP SALISBURY 74.10 DN SALISBURY
Miles from Waterloo reverse at 73.30

30A : to Southampton
81.76 Redbridge Jn
30A : to Totton

BML 2 S : LSW

23.37
23.13

Chandlers (UWC) 23.02
22.32

Banks (UWC)(NT) 21.51

CHANDLER'S FORD 75.25
M3 74.46

Chandler's Ford (UWC)(NT) 75.40

M27 21.42
Nursling (UWC)(NT)

[SW 130] ECR SR : LSW

'SALISBURY SINGLE'

UP
DN

Crawford (UWC)(NT) 78.40

Crammoor (UWC) 78.60

Halterworth (AHBC) 79.24
79.68

Romsey GF 80.50
80.35
80.47
ROMSEY (E)

UP TEST VALLEY
DOWN TEST VALLEY

[SW 150] RTJ 1 S : LSW

ECR 2 RTJ 1

Test River Bridge (20)
81.18 UP SALISBURY
DOWN SALISBURY

(SY) (E)

Tinwisions (UWC) 82.60
Terns (UWC) 82.30

Butler's (UWC) 83.06

MOTTISFONT & DUNBRIDGE (formerly DUNBRIDGE)
84.21

Dunbridge (UWC) 84.37
Kimbridge (AHBC-X) 84.24

Dean Hill (AHBC) 86.57

(SY) (E)
UP DEAN
DOWN DEAN

Controlled by Salisbury (SY)

Bishops (UWC) 86.13
East Dean (UWC)(NT) 87.40

DEAN 88.10

(AHBC) 88 14.11

RTJ 2 S : LSW
[SW 150] RTJ 2

Controlled by Eastleigh (E) ASC

Miles from Andover Jn via former Stockbridge line

Miles from Waterloo via Eastleigh (reverse)

32B

November 2008

© Copyright **TRACKmaps**. No reproduction without permission

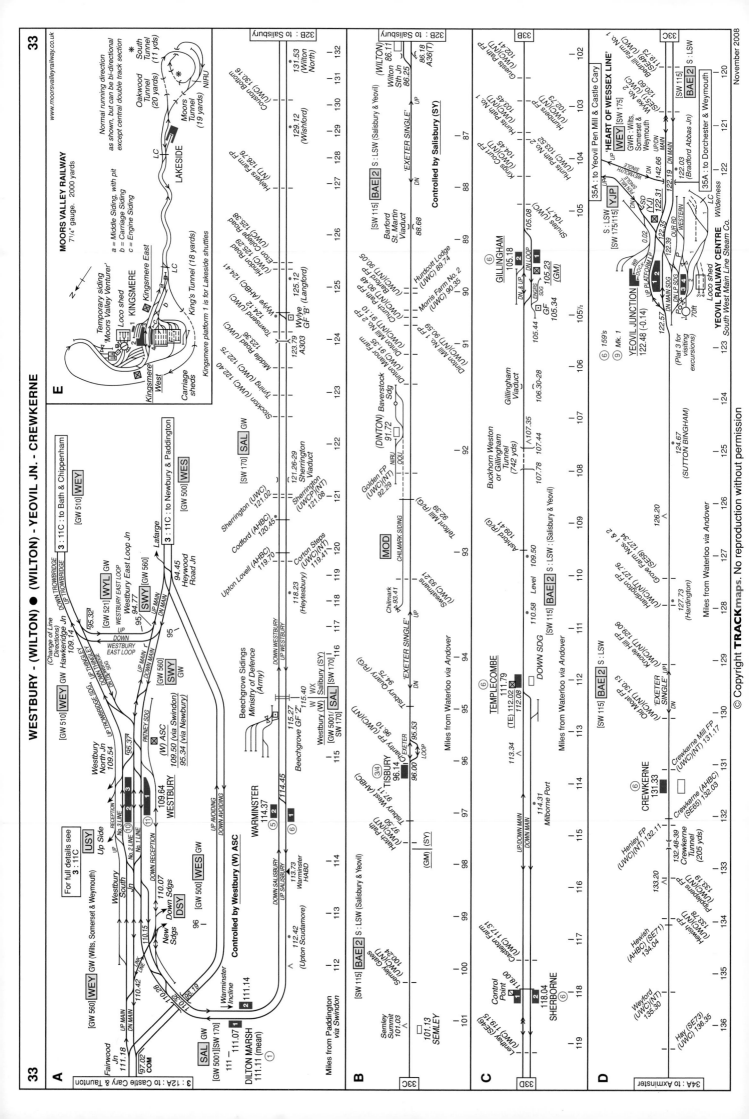

November 2008

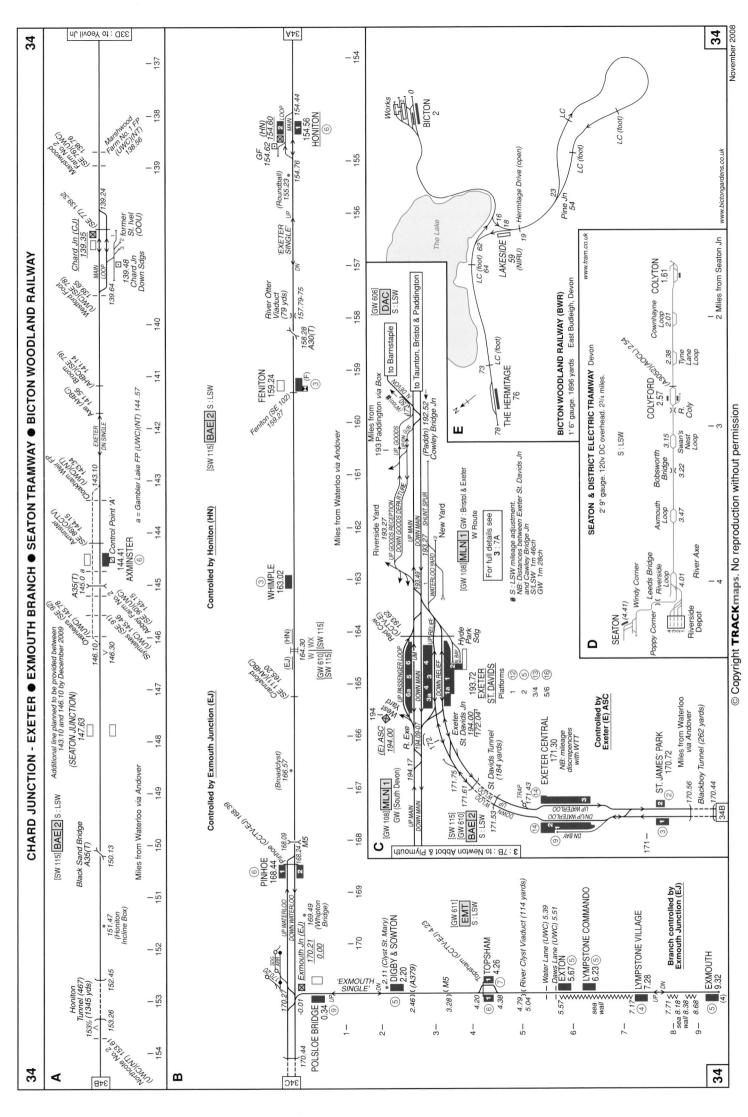

CHARD JUNCTION - EXETER ● EXMOUTH BRANCH ● SEATON TRAMWAY ● BICTON WOODLAND RAILWAY

November 2008

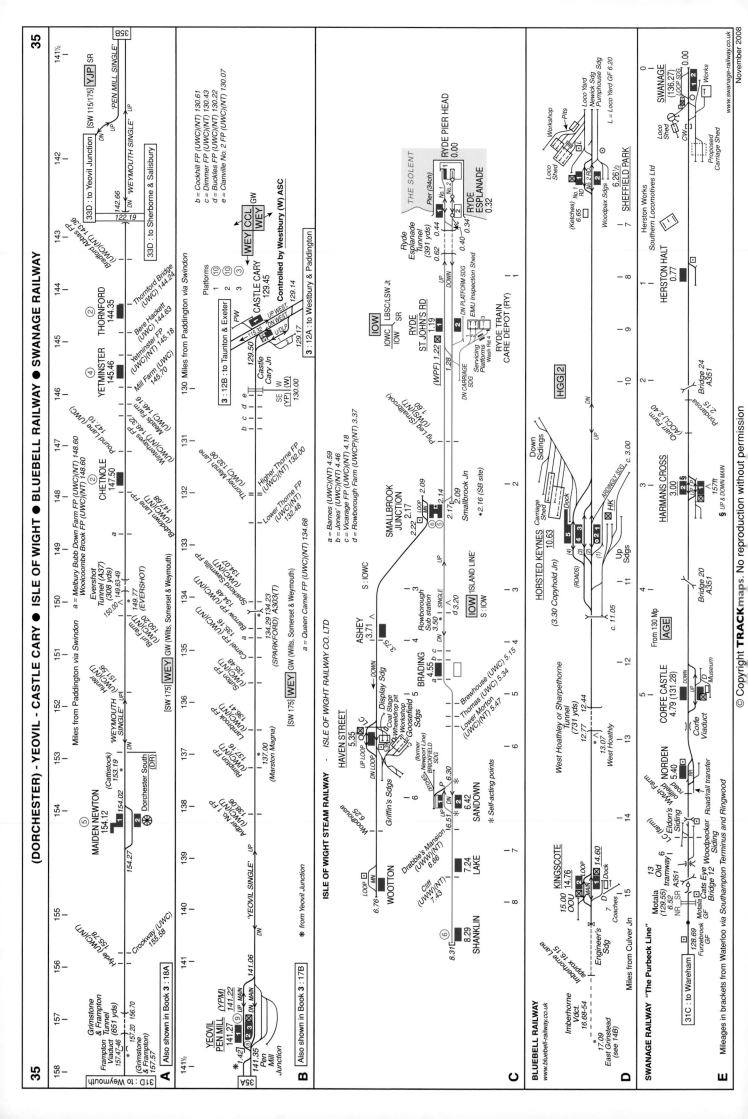

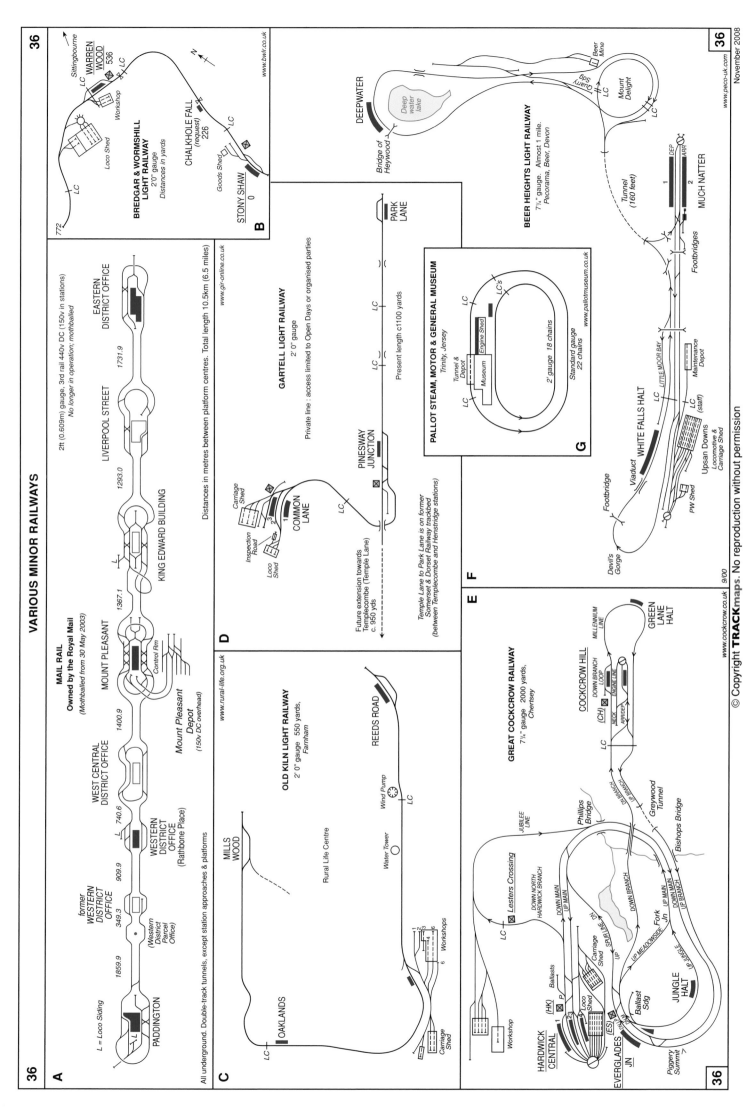

VARIOUS MINOR RAILWAYS

A

MAIL RAIL
Owned by the Royal Mail
(Mothballed from 30 May 2003)

2ft (0.609m) gauge, 3rd rail 440v DC (150v in stations)
No longer in operation; mothballed

EASTERN DISTRICT OFFICE

1731.9

LIVERPOOL STREET

1293.0

KING EDWARD BUILDING

1367.1

MOUNT PLEASANT

Control Rm

Mount Pleasant Depot
(150v DC overhead)

1400.9

WEST CENTRAL DISTRICT OFFICE

740.6

WESTERN DISTRICT OFFICE
(Rathbone Place)

909.9

former WESTERN DISTRICT OFFICE

349.3

(Western District Parcel Office)

1859.9

L

L = Loco Siding

PADDINGTON

All underground. Double-track tunnels, except station approaches & platforms

B

BREDGAR & WORMSHILL LIGHT RAILWAY
2'0" gauge
Distances in yards

to Sittingbourne

LC

WARREN WOOD 536

LC

Workshop

Loco Shed

LC

772

N

CHALKHOLE FALL (request) 226

LC

Goods Shed

STONY SHAW 0

www.bwlr.co.uk

DEEPWATER

Deep water lake

Bridge of Heywood

BEER HEIGHTS LIGHT RAILWAY
7¼" gauge. Almost 1 mile.
Pecorama, Beer, Devon.

Beer Mine

Quarry Sdg

Mount Delight

LC

LC

DEP

ARR

MUCH NATTER

1

2

Tunnel (160 feet)

Footbridges

LITTLE MOOR BAY

WHITE FALLS HALT

Maintenance Depot

LC (staff)

PW Shed

Locomotive & Carriage Shed

Upsan Downs

Viaduct

Footbridge

Devil's Gorge

www.peco-uk.com

November 2008

C

OLD KILN LIGHT RAILWAY
2'0" gauge 550 yards, Farnham

MILLS WOOD

Rural Life Centre

Water Tower

Wind Pump

LC

REEDS ROAD

OAKLANDS

LC

Carriage Shed

1 2 3 4 5 6

Workshops

www.rural-life.org.uk

D

GARTELL LIGHT RAILWAY
2'0" gauge

Private line : access limited to Open Days or organised parties

Present length c1100 yards

PARK LANE

LC

LC

LC

Carriage Shed

Inspection Road

Loco Shed

1 2 3

COMMON LANE

LC

PINESWAY JUNCTION

Future extension towards Templecombe (Temple Lane) c. 950 yds

Temple Lane to Park Lane is on former Somerset & Dorset Railway trackbed (between Templecombe and Henstridge stations)

www.gjr-online.co.uk

Distances in metres between platform centres. Total length 10.5km (6.5 miles)

G

PALLOT STEAM, MOTOR & GENERAL MUSEUM
Trinity, Jersey

Tunnel & Depot

Engine Shed

Museum

LC

LC's

LC

2' gauge 18 chains

Standard gauge 22 chains

www.pallotmuseum.co.uk

E F

GREAT COCKCROW RAILWAY
7¼" gauge 2000 yards, Chertsey

JUBILEE LINE

Lesters Crossing

LC

DOWN NORTH HARDWICK BRANCH

DOWN MAIN

UP MAIN

Phillips Bridge

SPUR LINE

UP

Carriage Shed

Fork Jn

UP MEADOWSIDE

DOWN MAIN

UP MAIN

DOWN BRANCH

UP BRANCH

UP JUNGLE

COCKCROW HILL

DOWN BRANCH LOOP

MILLENNIUM LINE

ENGINE LINE

NECK

ARRDEP

(CH)

LC

GREEN LANE HALT

Greywood Tunnel

Bishops Bridge

JUNGLE HALT

Ballast Sdg

Ballasts

P

Loco Shed

1 2 3

Workshop

HARDWICK CENTRAL (HK)

EVERGLADES JN (ES)

Piggery Summit

www.cockcrow.co.uk 9/00

© Copyright **TRACKmaps**. No reproduction without permission

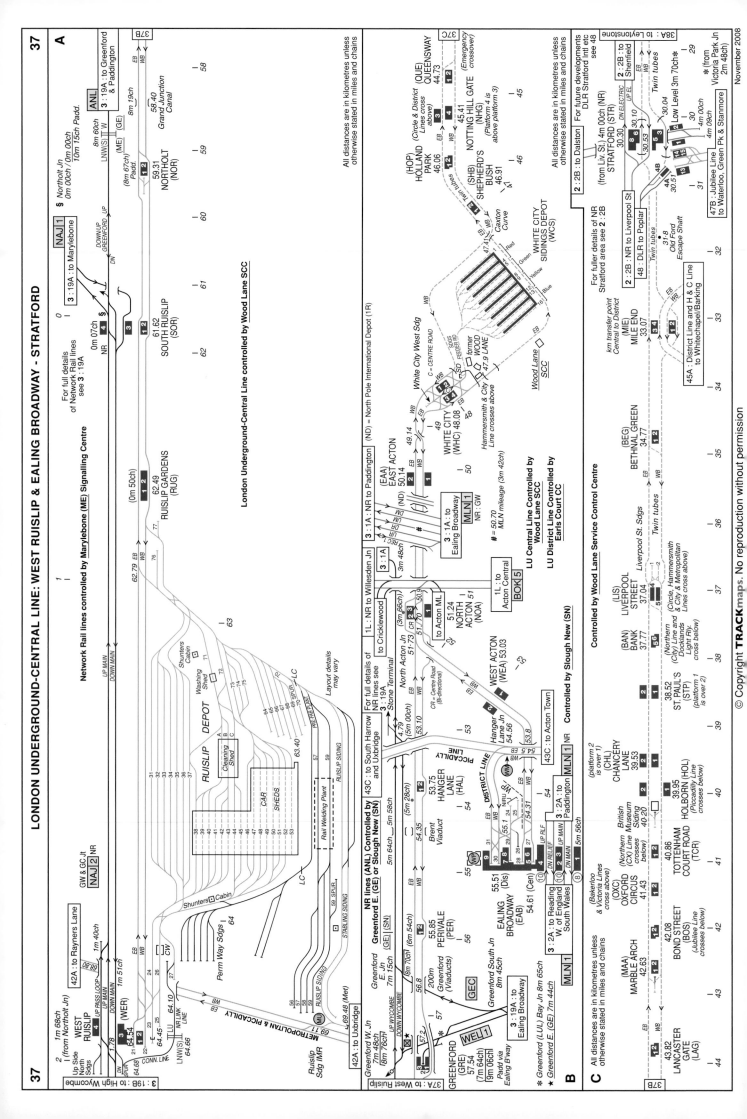

LONDON UNDERGROUND-CENTRAL LINE: WEST RUISLIP & EALING BROADWAY - STRATFORD

November 2008

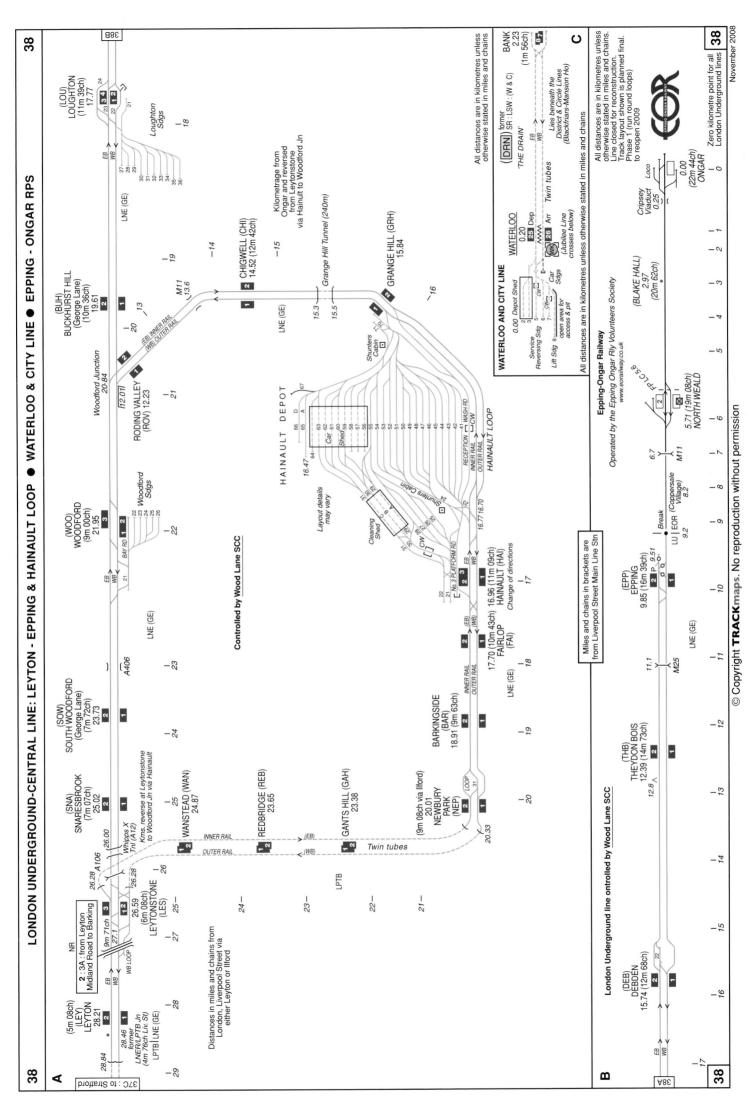

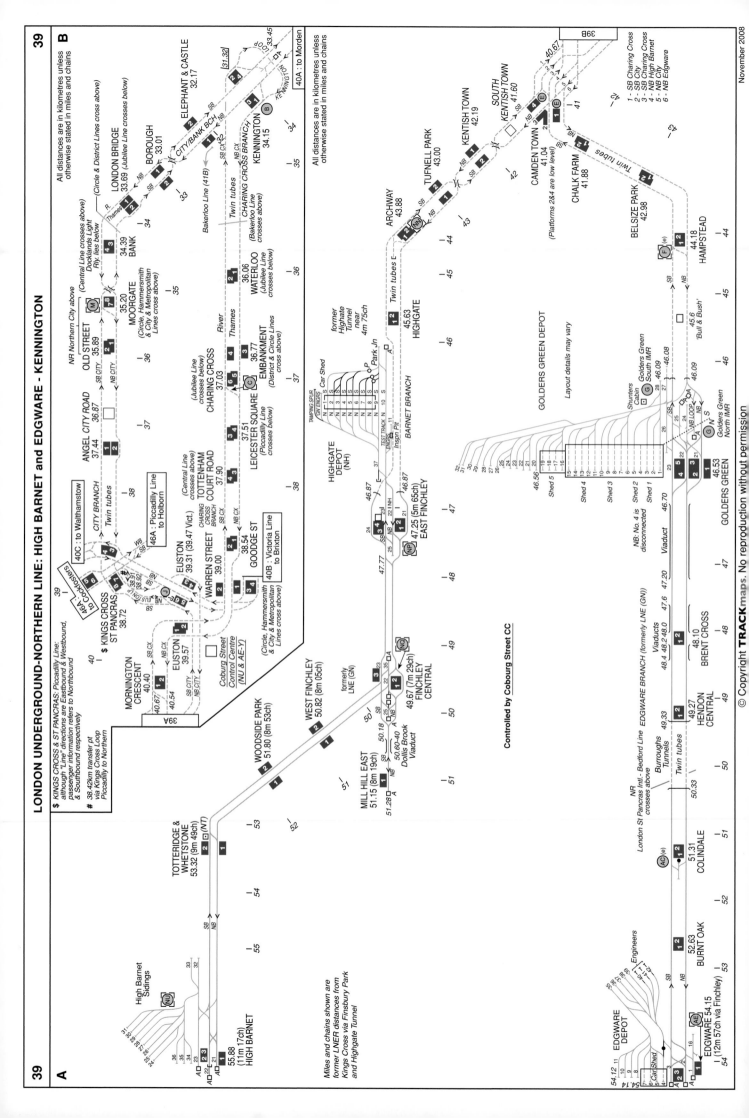

LONDON UNDERGROUND-NORTHERN LINE: HIGH BARNET and EDGWARE - KENNINGTON

All distances are in kilometres unless otherwise stated in miles and chains

$ KINGS CROSS & ST PANCRAS: Piccadilly Line: although "Line" directions are Eastbound & Westbound, passenger information refers to Northbound & Southbound respectively

38.42km transfer pt via Kings Cross Loop Piccadilly to Northern

All distances are in kilometres unless otherwise stated in miles and chains

Miles and chains shown are former LNER distances from Kings Cross via Finsbury Park and Highgate Tunnel

ELEPHANT & CASTLE 32.17
BOROUGH 33.01
LONDON BRIDGE 33.69 (Jubilee Line crosses below)
CITY/BANK BCH
KENNINGTON 34.15
CHARING CROSS BRANCH
Bakerloo Line (41B)
(Circle & District Lines cross above)
Docklands Light Rly lies below
(Central Line crosses above)

34.39 BANK

MOORGATE 35.20 (Circle, Hammersmith & City & Metropolitan Lines cross above)
OLD STREET 35.89
NR Northern City above
ANGEL CITY ROAD 36.87

WATERLOO 36.06 (Jubilee Line crosses below)
EMBANKMENT 36.77 (District & Circle Lines cross above)
CHARING CROSS 37.03 (Jubilee Line crosses below)
River Thames

LEICESTER SQUARE 37.51 (Piccadilly Line crosses below)
TOTTENHAM COURT ROAD 37.90 (Central Line crosses above)
CHARING CROSS BRANCH

GOODGE ST 38.54
WARREN STREET 39.00
EUSTON 39.31 (39.47 Vict.)
CITY BRANCH
Twin tubes

KINGS CROSS ST PANCRAS 38.72
EUSTON 39.57
MORNINGTON CRESCENT 40.40

Coburg Street Control Centre (NU & AE-Y)

40C : to Walthamstow
46A : Piccadilly Line to Holborn
40B : Victoria Line to Brixton

TUFNELL PARK 43.00
ARCHWAY 43.88
KENTISH TOWN 42.19
SOUTH KENTISH TOWN 41.60
CAMDEN TOWN 41.04
CHALK FARM 41.88
BELSIZE PARK 42.98
HAMPSTEAD 44.18

Twin tubes
(Platforms 2&4 are low level)

HIGHGATE 45.63
former Highgate Tunnel near 4m 75ch

HIGHGATE DEPOT (NH)
TAMPING SPUR
GN ENGRS Car Shed
TEST TRACK
Inspn Pit
Park Jn

BARNET BRANCH
EAST FINCHLEY 47.25 (5m 65ch)
46.87

FINCHLEY CENTRAL 49.67 (7m 29ch)
formerly LNE (GN)

WEST FINCHLEY 50.82 (8m 05ch)
WOODSIDE PARK 51.80 (8m 53ch)
MILL HILL EAST 51.15 (8m 19ch)
Dollis Brook Viaduct

TOTTERIDGE & WHETSTONE 53.32 (9m 49ch)

HIGH BARNET 55.88 (11m 17ch)
High Barnet Sidings

GOLDERS GREEN DEPOT
Layout details may vary
Shunters Cabin
Golders Green South IMR
Golders Green North IMR
NB LOOP
Golders Green 46.53
NB: No. 4 is disconnected
Shed 5, Shed 4, Shed 3, Shed 2, Shed 1
Viaduct

Controlled by Cobourg Street CC

'Bull & Bush'

NR London St Pancras Intl. - Bedford Line crosses above
EDGWARE BRANCH (formerly LNE (GN))

BRENT CROSS 48.10
HENDON CENTRAL 49.27
Viaducts 48.4 48.2 48.0
Burroughs Tunnels
Twin tubes

COLINDALE 51.31
BURNT OAK 52.63
Engineers
EDGWARE 54.15 (12m 57ch via Finchley)
EDGWARE DEPOT
Car Shed

1 - SB Charing Cross
2 - SB City
3 - SB Charing Cross
4 - NB High Barnet
5 - NB City
6 - NB Edgware

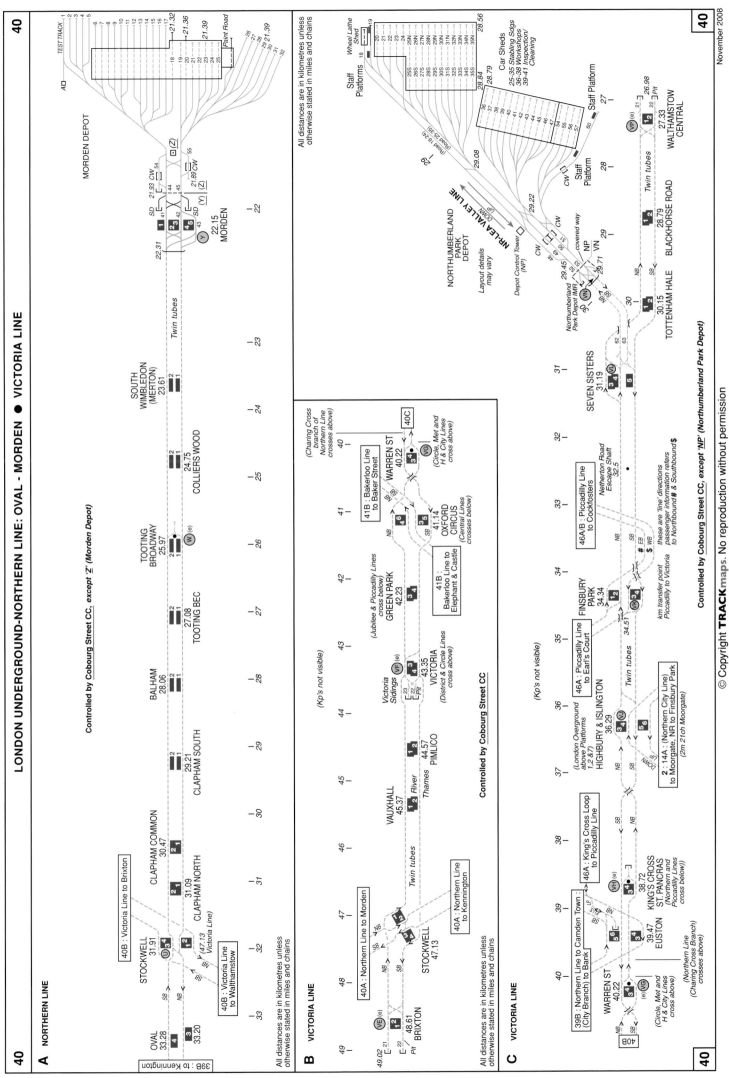

A NORTHERN LINE

Controlled by Cobourg Street CC, except 'Z' (Morden Depot)

TEST TRACK

MORDEN DEPOT

Paint Road

All distances are in kilometres unless otherwise stated in miles and chains

21.32
21.36
21.39
21.39

SD 21.93 CW
21.89 CW

MORDEN 22.15

SOUTH WIMBLEDON (MERTON) 23.61

COLLIERS WOOD 24.75

Twin tubes

TOOTING BROADWAY 25.97

TOOTING BEC 27.08

BALHAM 28.06

CLAPHAM SOUTH 29.21

CLAPHAM COMMON 30.47

CLAPHAM NORTH 31.09

40B : Victoria Line to Brixton

STOCKWELL 31.91

(47.13) Victoria Line

40B : Victoria Line to Walthamstow

OVAL 33.28

39B : to Kennington

B VICTORIA LINE

All distances are in kilometres unless otherwise stated in miles and chains

(Kp's not visible)

(Charing Cross branch of Northern Line crosses above)

WARREN ST 40.22

40C

41B : Bakerloo Line to Baker Street

(Circle, Met and H & City Lines cross above)

OXFORD CIRCUS (Central Lines crosses below) 41.14

(Jubilee & Piccadilly Lines cross below)

GREEN PARK 42.23

41B : Bakerloo Line to Elephant & Castle

VICTORIA (District & Circle Lines cross above) 43.35

Victoria Sidings

PIMLICO 44.57

VAUXHALL 45.37

River Thames

Twin tubes

40A : Northern Line to Morden

40A : Northern Line to Kennington

STOCKWELL 47.13

Controlled by Cobourg Street CC

BRIXTON 48.61 49.02

All distances are in kilometres unless otherwise stated in miles and chains

C VICTORIA LINE

(Kp's not visible)

(London Overground above Platforms 1,2 & 7!)

HIGHBURY & ISLINGTON 36.29

2 : 14A : (Northern City Line) to Moorgate, NR to Finsbury Park (2m 21ch Moorgate)

46A : Piccadilly Line to Earl's Court

km transfer point Piccadilly to Victoria

FINSBURY PARK 34.34 34.51

46A/B : Piccadilly Line to Cockfosters

Netherton Road Escape Shaft 32.5

these are 'line' directions passenger information refers to Northbound # & Southbound$

$ EB WB

SEVEN SISTERS 31.19

TOTTENHAM HALE 30.15

NR LEA VALLEY LINE UP DOWN

Northumberland Park Depot IMR 29.45 29.71

BLACKHORSE ROAD 28.79

WALTHAMSTOW CENTRAL 27.33 26.98

Twin tubes

NORTHUMBERLAND PARK DEPOT

Depot Control Tower (NP)

Layout details may vary

covered way

All distances are in kilometres unless otherwise stated in miles and chains

Wheel Lathe Shed

Staff Platforms

Car Sheds

25-35 Stabling Sdgs
36-38 Workshops
39-41 Inspection/ Cleaning

Staff Platform

Staff Platform

28.56

28.84 28.79

29.08

(Road 19-24)

(Road 25-35)

Controlled by Cobourg Street CC, except 'NP' (Northumberland Park Depot)

39B : Northern Line to Camden Town : (City Branch) to Bank

(Northern Line (Charing Cross Branch) crosses above)

WARREN ST 40.22

(Circle, Met and H & City Lines cross above)

40B

KING'S CROSS ST. PANCRAS (Northern and Piccadilly Lines cross below) 38.72

EUSTON 39.47

46A : King's Cross Loop to Piccadilly Line

© Copyright TRACKmaps. No reproduction without permission

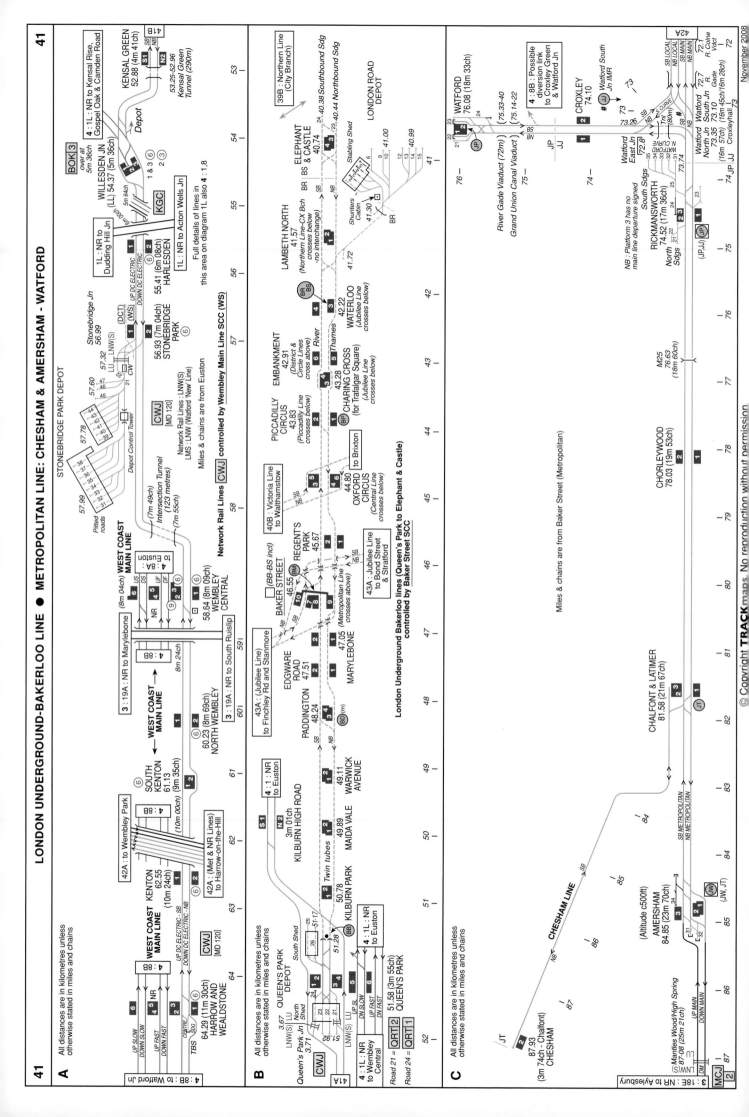

LONDON UNDERGROUND-METROPOLITAN LINE: MOOR PARK & UXBRIDGE - (FINCHLEY ROAD) ● JUBILEE LINE: STANMORE - WEST HAMPSTEAD

A

All distances are in kilometres unless otherwise stated in miles and chains

Jubilee Line controlled by Baker Street : Metropolitan & Jubilee SSC

41A : **4** : **8B** : NR to Harrow & Wealdstone
41A: Harrow-on-the-Hill to Queens Park
4 : **8B** : NR to Euston

41A : Bakerloo Line to Queens Park
* Miles from former Manchester London Road via Former GC Main Line

PRESTON ROAD 58.84
KINGSBURY 60.23
NORTHWICK PARK 60.49
QUEENSBURY 61.56
HARROW-ON-THE-HILL 60.1 / 61.78
CANONS PARK 63.27
JUBILEE LINE
WEST HARROW 63.03
NORTH HARROW 63.77
Harrow North Jn 62.83
STANMORE 64.62
(11m 19ch) Baker St (Met)
Stanmore Sidings
PINNER 65.25
RAYNERS LANE 64.41
Rayners Lane Jn 64.33
43C : to Acton Town (Piccadilly line)
EASTCOTE 66.14
(16m 30ch Mansion House)
NORTHWOOD HILLS 67.33
RUISLIP MANOR 67.28
RUISLIP 68.00
NORTHWOOD 68.95
(15m 28ch Baker St)
37A : to W. Ruislip
LU Central : **3** : **19A** : NR
37A : to S. Ruislip
to Ruislip Depot : 37A : to S. Ruislip
ICKENHAM 69.85
A = spur road/rail vehicle transfer point
MOOR PARK 71.16
METROPOLITAN &
PICCADILLY LINES
HILLINGDON (Swakeleys) 70.93
41C : to Watford & Amersham
* (6m 71ch) Harrow Jn (Met)
Uxbridge Sidings
UXBRIDGE 73.03
Uxbridge 72.30

LONDON UNDERGROUND DISTANCES
(from June 1972)

Distances are measured in kilometres from an origin 0.000 at the former terminus at Ongar. Distances, denoted with posts/plates every 0.2km, proceed westwards along the Central line to its termini at West Ruislip and Ealing Broadway. Distances on other lines are calculated via the following 'transfer locations' from which measurements may increase or decrease.

From Line	To Line	Transfer Point	Distance
Central	District	Mile End	33.1
District	Piccadilly	Barons Court	47.8
Piccadilly	Metropolitan	Rayners Lane	64.4
Piccadilly	Victoria	Finsbury Park	34.4
Piccadilly	Northern	King's Cross loop	38.4
Metropolitan	Jubilee	Finchley Road	50.1
Jubilee	Bakerloo	Baker Street	46.5

B

All distances are in kilometres unless otherwise stated in miles and chains

LU Lines controlled by Baker Street : Metropolitan & Jubilee SCC
NR Lines controlled by Marylebone ASC (3 : 18C)

* Miles from former Manchester London Road via Former GC Main Line

NEASDEN DEPOT
Layout details may vary
South End
North End
Neasden Service Control Centre for Jubilee Line Extension only (Green Park) to Stratford
Chemical Washing Shed
Car Sheds
Klondyke Sidings
Wheel Monitoring Shed
Permanent Way Sdgs
Neasden Depot Train Movements Room

NEASDEN 55.09 / 55.07
Neasden Sth Jn
ø (6m 31ch) from Northolt Jn
* 200m 66ch
1L : to Neasden Jn
1L : to Neasden Jn & Acton Wells Jn
1L : to South Ruislip
1L : to Neasden Freight Terminal
METROPOLITAN SB FAST
JUBILEE SB
METROPOLITAN NB FAST
JUBILEE NB
UP HARROW
DOWN HARROW

NR **MCJ1** [MD 701] LNE : GC

WEMBLEY PARK 57.38
(6m 59ch) Baker Street (Met)
Wembley Park Reversing Sidings
MET SB F / MET SB LOCAL / JUB SB LOCAL / JUB NB LOCAL / MET NB LOCAL / MET NB FAST
UP HARROW / DOWN HARROW
Flyunder / Flyover

43A : to Finchley Rd
WEST HAMPSTEAD 50.75
KILBURN 51.84
WILLESDEN GREEN 53.03
DOLLIS HILL 54.80 / 54.24
4 : **1R** : NR to Gospel Oak
4 : **1L** : NR to Willesden Jn
1L : NR to Cricklewood
JUBILEE SB / JUBILEE NB / UP MAIN / DOWN MAIN
201m 09ch

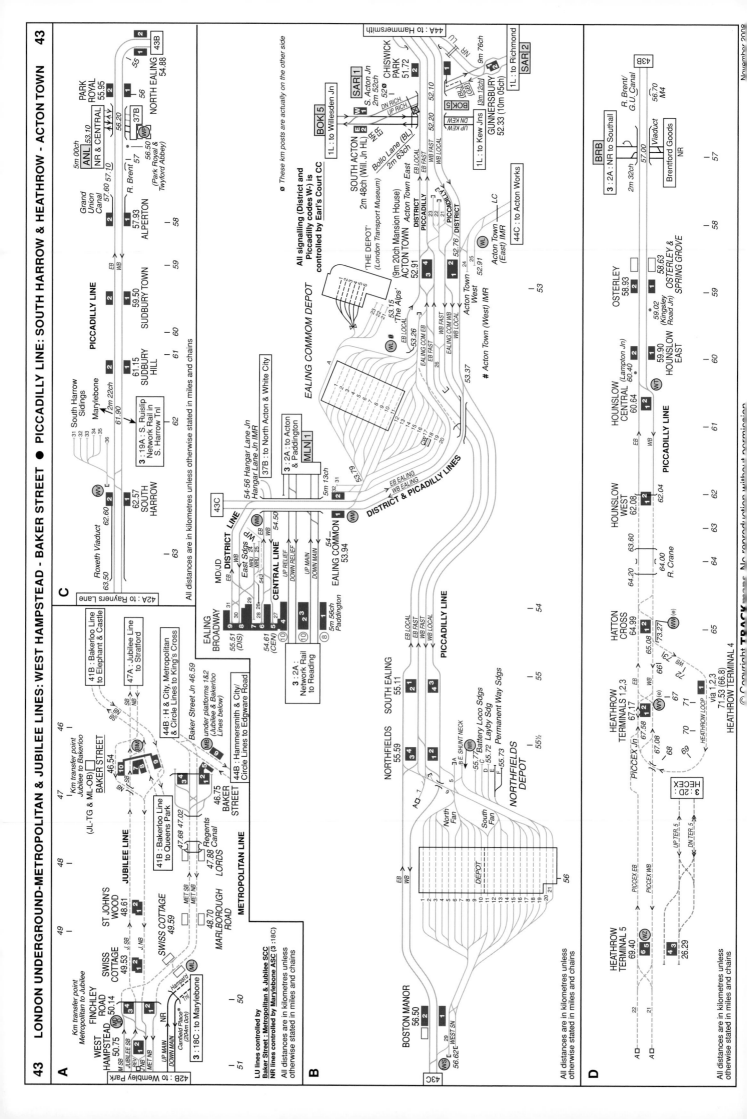

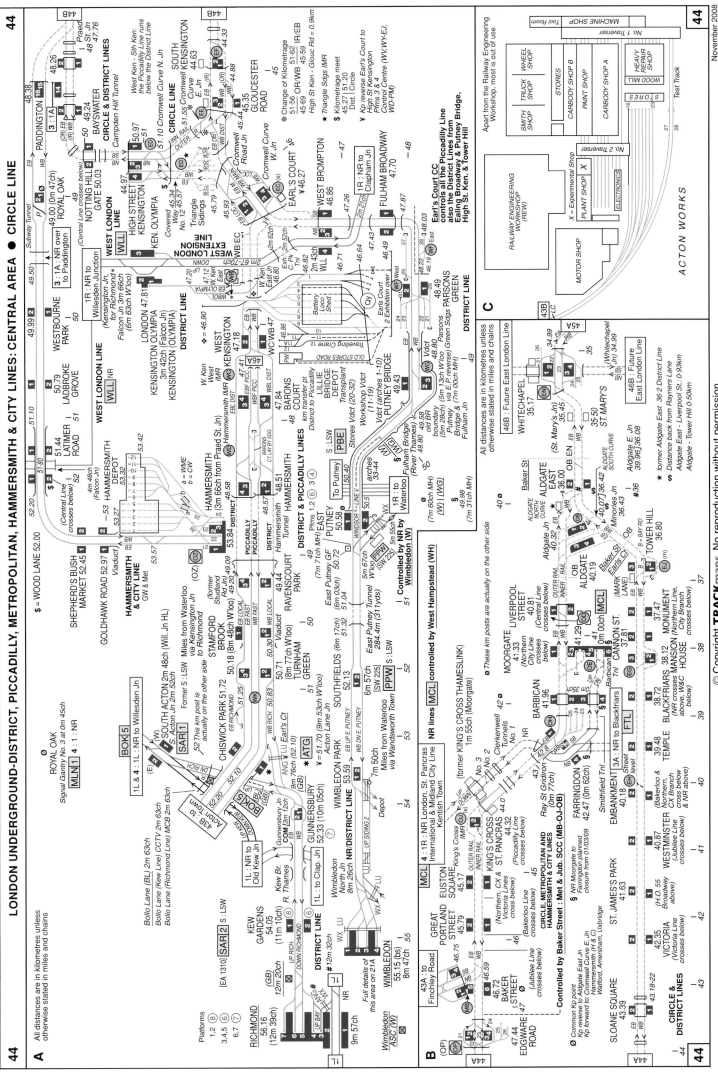

November 2008

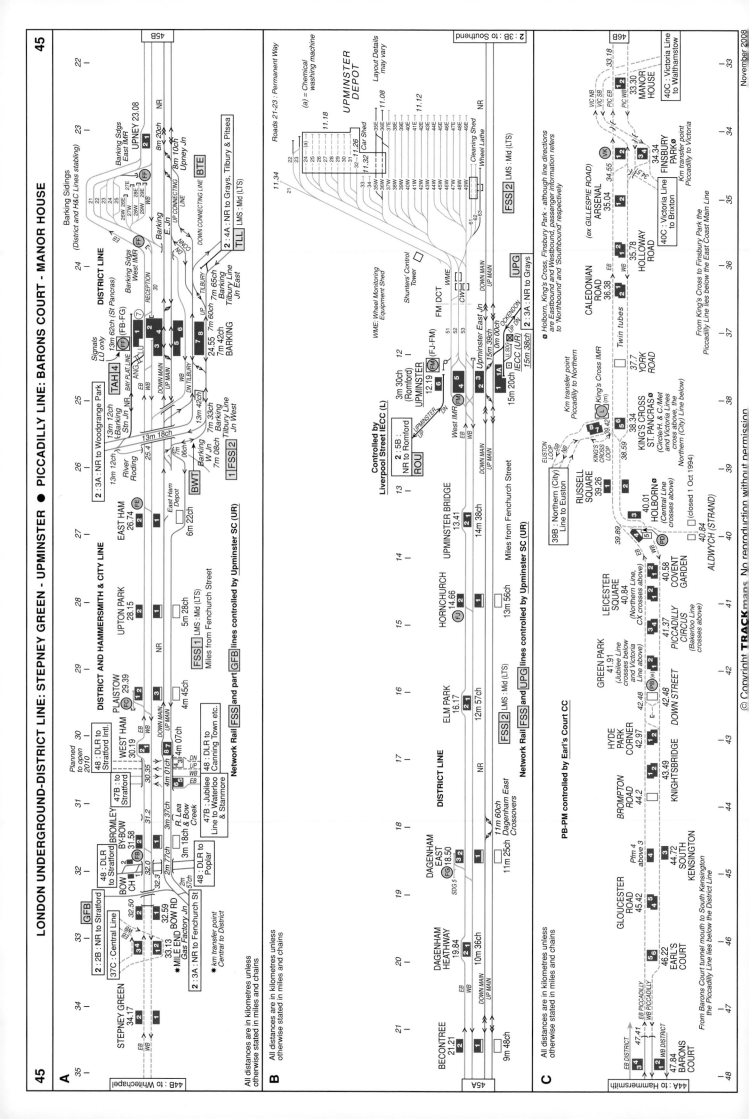

LONDON UNDERGROUND-PICCADILLY LINE: COCKFOSTERS ● EAST LONDON LINE

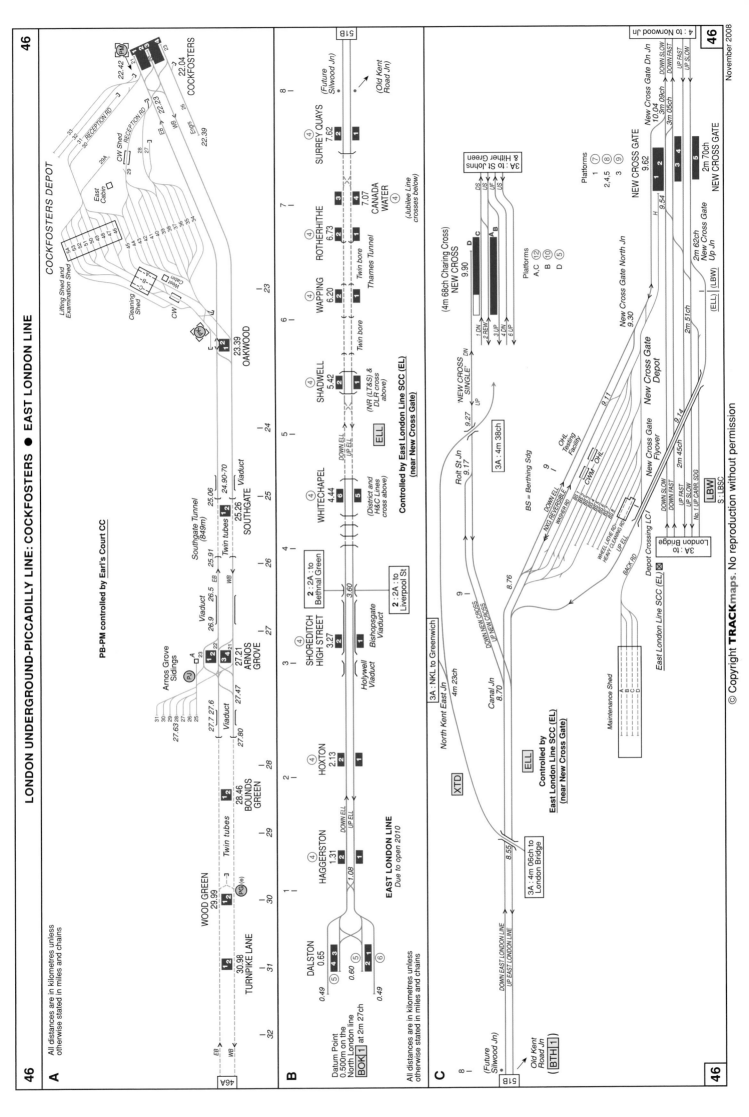

November 2008

All distances are in kilometres unless otherwise stated in miles and chains

A

COCKFOSTERS DEPOT

PB-PM controlled by Earl's Court CC

B

EAST LONDON LINE
Due to open 2010

All distances are in kilometres unless otherwise stated in miles and chains

Controlled by East London Line SCC (EL)
(near New Cross Gate)

C

Controlled by East London Line SCC (EL)
(near New Cross Gate)

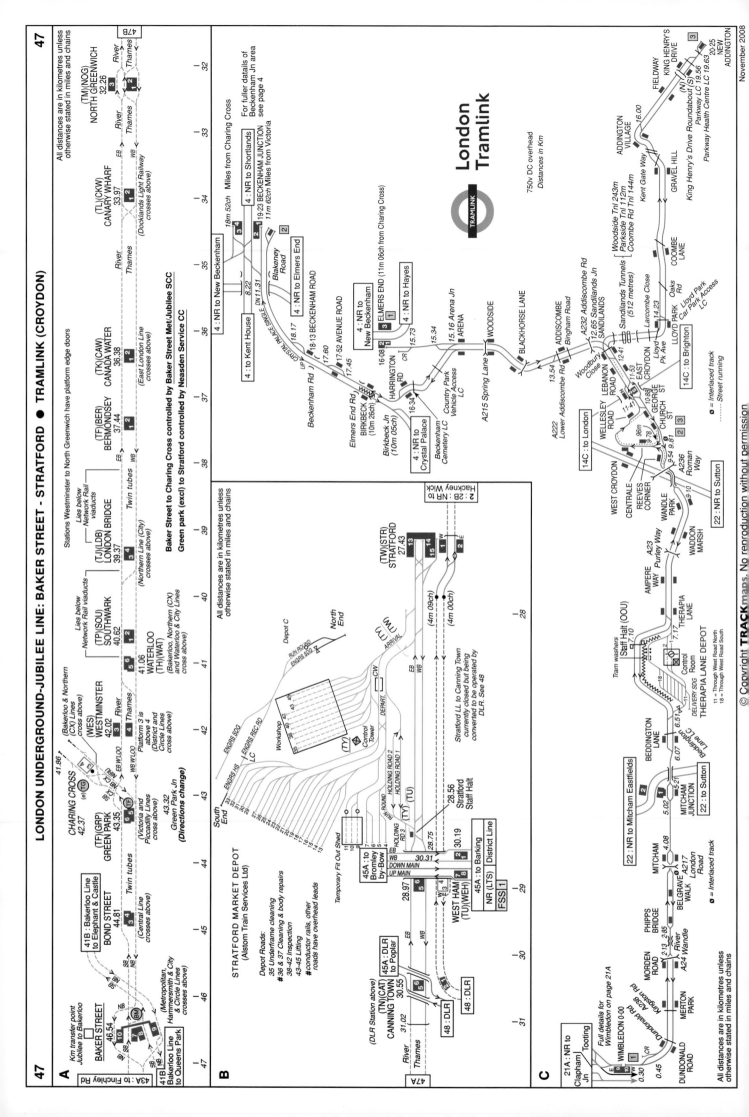

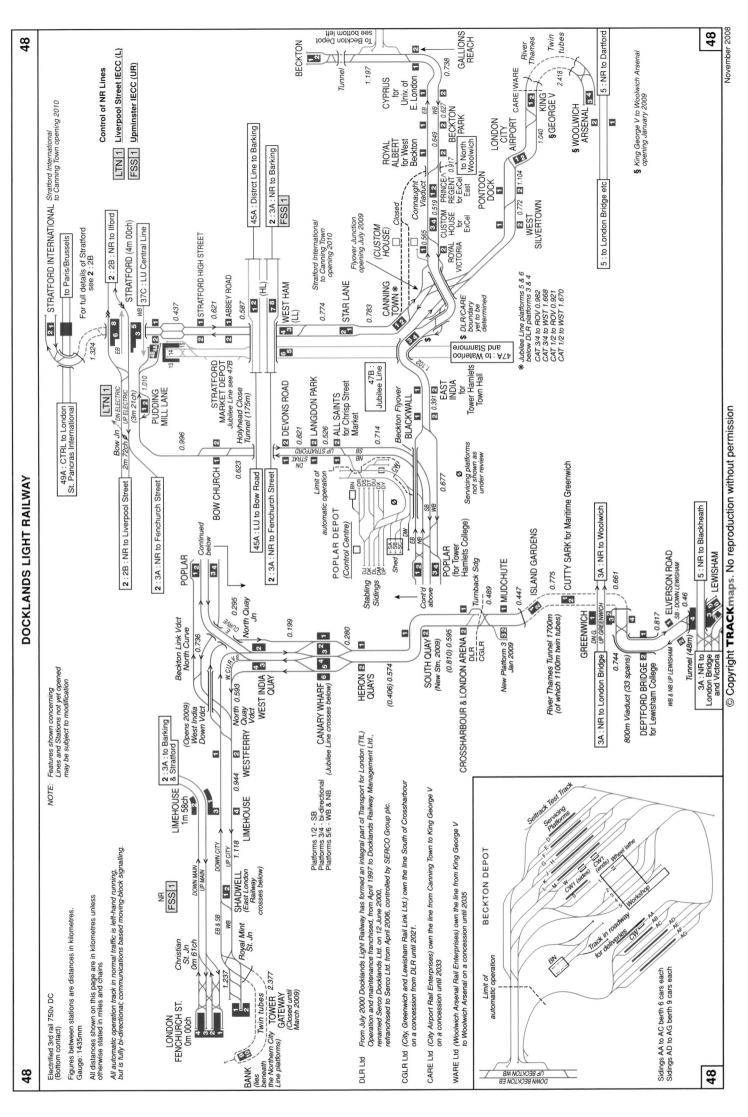

DOCKLANDS LIGHT RAILWAY

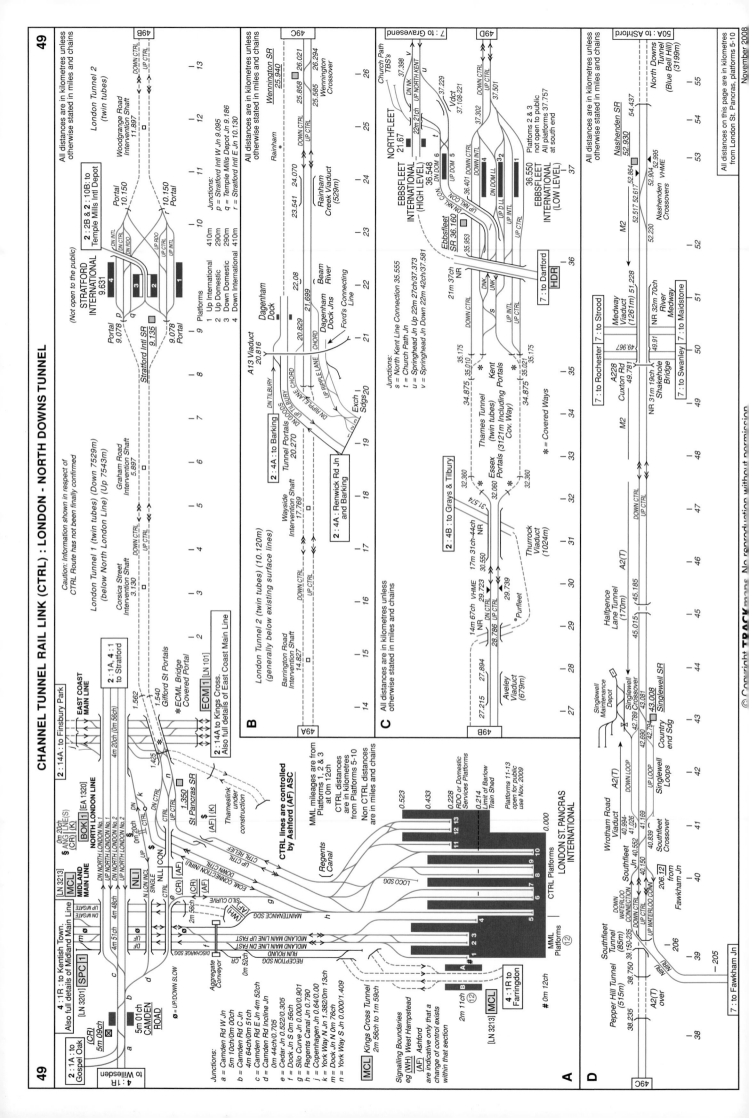

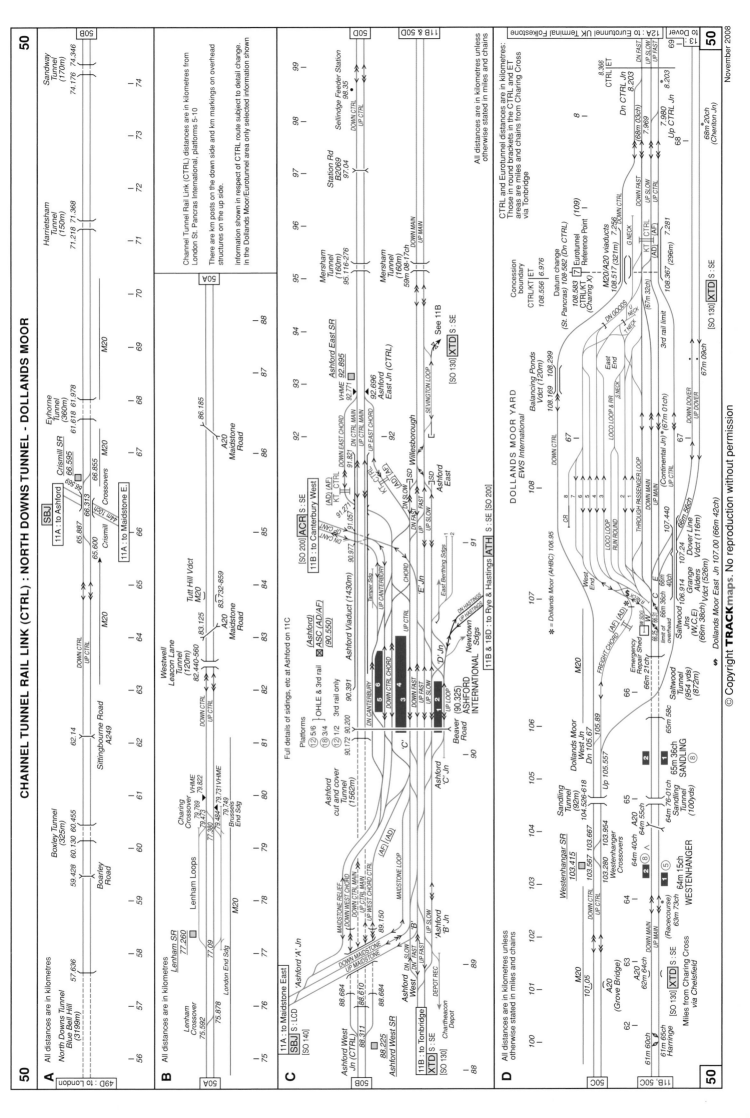

CHANNEL TUNNEL RAIL LINK (CTRL) : NORTH DOWNS TUNNEL - DOLLANDS MOOR

November 2008

Index

In the creation of the index, the full listing of locations and assets was subjected was subjected to a mild cull, made to arbitrary rules. The vast majority remain to assist the reader in searching the Maps, including the locations of now-defunct assets (given in brackets) and most level crossings. The approaches to the London termini include over 130 viaducts and arches which are named on the maps but excluded from the Index. Generally, private and preserved railways are limited to the main title (in *italics*) or, in some cases, the main stations.

Location	Ref
Blue Pigeon LC (UWC)	9A
BLUEBELL RAILWAY	35D
Boarmans LC	18D
BODIAM (KESR)	13A
BOGNOR REGIS	20C
Bognor Regis SB (BR)	20C
Bollo Lane LC (Kew Line) (CCTV)	1L
Bollo Lane SB (BL)	43B, 44A
Bollo Lane SB (CCTV)	1L
Bollo Lane SB LC (BL) (MCB)	1L
BOND STREET	37C, 47A
BOOKHAM	22
Bookham Tunnel	22
Bo-Peep Jn	17B, 18C
Bo-Peep Jn SB (BJ)	17B, 18C
Bo-Peep Tunnel	17B, 18C
BOROUGH	39B
BOROUGH GREEN & WROTHAM	7
(Borough Market Jn)	3A
(Boscombe)	31A
BOSHAM	20D
Bosham LC (AHBC)	20D
BOSTON MANOR	43B
BOTLEY	28B
Botley Viaduct	28B
BOUNDS GREEN	46A
BOURNEMOUTH	31A
BOW CHURCH (DLR)	48
BOW JN (DLR)	48
BOW ROAD	45A
Bowdell LC	18D
Bowermans LC (UWC)	20B
BOXHILL & WESTHUMBLE	19A, 22
Boxley Tunnel	50A
BRACKNELL	25B
Bradford Abbas LC (FP)(UWC)	35A
Bradford Peverell Viaduct	31D
BRADING	35C
BRAMLEY	27A
Bramley LC (AHBC)	27A
(Bramshott)	24C
BRANKSOME	31A
Branksome Jn	31A
Branksome Viaduct	31A
Brasted Lands LC (UWC)	10A
BREDGAR & WORMSHILL LIGHT RLY	36B
BRENT CROSS	39A
Brent Cross Viaducts	39A
Brent Curve Jn	1L
Brent Viaduct	37B
BRENTFORD	1L
Brewhouse LC (UWC)	35C
Bricklayers Arms Jn	3A
BRIGHTON	16
British Museum Sdg (LU)	37C
BRIXTON	3A, 4, 40B
Brixton Jn	3A, 4
Broad Oak LC (AHBC)	9B
(Broadclyst)	34B
BROADSTAIRS	9A
BROCKENHURST	30B
Brockenhurst Jn	30B
Brockenhurst SB (BH)	30B
BROCKLEY	3A, 4
(Brockley Lane)	3, 4
Bromley Down Jn	4
BROMLEY NORTH	3B
BROMLEY SOUTH	6A
Bromley Up Jn	4
BROMLEY-BY-BOW	45A
Brompton Road	45C
Brook Lane LC (UWC) (Angmering)	20B
Brook Lane LC (UWC) (Bosham)	20D
Brook LC (AHBC)	24A
Brookbarn LC	20C
Brookgate Sidings	7
Brookham LC (AHBC)	24A
Brookland LC (AOCL)	18D
Brooks Lance LC (FP)(UWC)	19B
BROOKWOOD	23
Broom LC (AHBC)	34A
Bubdown Lane LC (FP)(UWC)	35A
Buckhorn Weston/Gillingham Tunnel	33C
BUCKHURST HILL	38A
Buckland Junction	13
Buckland LC (AHBC)	15A, 24B
Buckles LC (FP)(UWC)	35B
Buckwell LC (UWC)(NT)	11B
Bull & Bush	39A
(Bungalow Town, Shoreham Airport)	20A
BURGESS HILL	15C
Buriton LC (FP)(UWC)	26B
Buriton Tunnel	26B
Burl Farm LC (UWC)	35A
BURNT OAK	39A
Burroughs Tunnels	39A
Burrows Lane LC (AHBC)	24A
BURSLEDON	29
Burton Common LC (FP)(UWC)	31B
Butler's LC (UWC)	32C
BUXTED	14A
BYFLEET & NEW HAW	21B
Byfleet Jn	21B
Cabul Road (Latchmere) Viaduct	1R
Cadland (E. Avenue) LC	30A
Cadlands	30A
CALAIS-FRÉTHUN	12D
Caldicott LC	18D
CALEDONIAN ROAD	45C
CAMBERLEY	24C
Camberley LC (CCTV)	24C
(CAMBERWELL)	3A
Cambria Jn	3A
Cambria Jn	4
CAMDEN ROAD	49A
CAMDEN TOWN	39A
Camel LC (FP)(UWC)	35B
Campden Hill Tunnel (LU)	44A
CANADA WATER (East London Line)	46B
CANADA WATER (Jubilee Line)	47A
Canal Jn	3A
Canal Jn (New Cross)	46C
CANARY WHARF	47A
CANARY WHARF (DLR)	48
Cane Hill Cutting	14C
CANNING TOWN	47B
CANNING TOWN (DLR)	48
CANNON STREET	44B
CANONS PARK	42A
CANTERBURY EAST	9B
Canterbury East SB (CB)	9B
Canterbury Road Jn	3A, 4
Canterbury Viaduct	9B
CANTERBURY WEST	9B
Canterbury West SB (EBT)	9B
Canterbury West SB (EDH)	9B
Canute Road LC (AOCL)	29
Carlisle Lane Jn	2R
CARSHALTON	22
CARSHALTON BEECHES	22
CASTLE CARY	35B
Castle Cary Jn	35B
Castle Hill Portal	12A
Castleton Farm LC (UWC)	33C
Cater LC (UWC)	9A
CATERHAM	14C
CATFORD	4
CATFORD BRIDGE	4
(Cattistock)	35A
CEGB LC (UWC)	18A
CENTRAL LINE	37, 38, 43B
CENTRALE (Tramlink)	14C, 47
CHALFONT & LATIMER	41C
CHALK FARM	39A
Chalk Tunnel	23, 26A
Chalkwell LC (UWC)	7
CHANCERY LANE	37C
CHANDLERS FORD	32C
Chandlers Ford LC (UWC)	32C
Chandlers LC (UWC)	32C
Chantry LC (FP)UWC)	33B
CHAPEL ROAD	29
Chapel Road LC (AOCL)	29
Chard Jn Down Sidings	34A
Chard Jn SB (CJ)	34A
Chard Junction	34A
CHARING	11A
CHARING CROSS	39B, 41B, 47A
Charing Crossover	50B
CHARLTON	5
Charlton Jn	5
Charlton Lane LC	5
Charlton Tunnel	13
Chart LC (UWC)	10D
CHARTHAM	9B
Chartham Hatch LC (AHBC)	9B
Chartham LC (MG)	9B
Chartham Sidgs (Canterbury)	9B
CHATHAM	8A
Chatham Dockyard	8A
CHATHAM HISTORIC DOCKYARD RAILWAY	8D
Chatham Tunnel	8A
CHEAM	22
Chelsea Bridge (R. Thames)	1R, 2L
CHELSFIELD	6A
Chelsfield Tunnel	6A
Cheriton Jn	12A
(Cheriton Jn)	11C, 50D
Cheriton Tunnel	12A
CHERTSEY	25A
Chertsey LC (CCTV)	25A
CHESHAM	41C
CHESSINGTON NORTH	22
CHESSINGTON SOUTH	22
CHESTFIELD & SWALECLIFFE	9A
CHETNOLE	35A
CHICHESTER	20D
Chichester SB (CC)	20D
Chicknal Sidings	28A
Chicks Farm (Stratton) LC (UWC)	31D
Chicks Farm Foot LC (UWC)	31D
CHIGWELL	38A
CHILHAM	11B
Chilham Mill LC (CCTV)	11B
Chilham Road LC (CCTV)	11B
Chilmark	33B
CHILWORTH	24A
Chilworth LC (CCTV)	24A
CHIPSTEAD	14C
Chipstead Viaduct	14C
CHISLEHURST	3B, 6A
Chislehurst Jn	6A
Chislehurst Tunnels	3B
CHISLET COLLIERY	9A
(Chislet Colliery SB)	9A
CHISWICK	1L
CHISWICK PARK	43B, 44A
CHORLEYWOOD	41C
CHRISTCHURCH	31A
Christian St. Jn (DLR)	48
Christian Street Jn	48
CHRIST'S HOSPITAL	19C
Church Lane Jn	29
Church Lane LC (UWC)	7
Church LC (FP)(UWC) (Wateringbury)	10C
Church LC (FP)(UWC) (Southbourne)	20D
Church Path Jn	49C
Church Path LC (FP)(UWC)	33B
CHURCH STREET (Tramlink)	14C, 47C
Churchfield Road LC (CCTV)	1L
CIRCLE LINE	44B
City Road	39B
CITY THAMESLINK	3A
CLANDON	23
Clanville No.2 LC (UWC)	35B
CLAPHAM COMMON	40A
CLAPHAM HIGH STREET	2R
CLAPHAM JUNCTION	1R, 2L, 4
CLAPHAM NORTH	40A
CLAPHAM SOUTH	40A
Clapham West London Jn	2L
Clapham Yard	1R, 2L
Clarendon Park Viaduct	32B
Clay Lane LC (AHBC)	20D
CLAYGATE	22
Clayton Tunnel	15C
Clerkenwell Tunnels (LU)	44B
Cliff LC (UWW)(UWC)	35C
(Cliffe)	5
Cliffsend LC (AHBC)	9A
Cliftonville Tunnel	16
CLOCK HOUSE	4
Clock House LC (AHBC)	8B
Clookham West LC (FP)(UWC)	34A
COBHAM & STOKE D'ABERNON	22
Cobourg Street Control Centre	39B
COCKFOSTERS	46A
Cockfosters Depot (LU)	46A
Cockhill LC (FP)(UWC)	35B
Codford LC	33A
Cold Blow LC (R/G)	13
Coldharbour LC	18D
Colemans LC (UWC)	31B
COLINDALE	39A
COLLIERS WOOD	40A
COLLINGTON	17B
Connaught Viaduct (DLR)	48
(Continental Jn)	50D
COODEN BEACH	17B
Cookes LC (UWC)	18D
Cooks LC (CCTV)	22
Cooks No.1 LC (UWC)	18D
COOKSBRIDGE	15C, 16
Cooksbridge LC (CCTV)	15C, 16
Cookspond Viaduct	14B
COOMBE LANE (Tramlink)	47C
Coombe Lane Lane LC (UWC)	24B
Coopers & Farmers LC (UWC)	18C
Coopers Hill Viaduct	10A
Coopers LC (UWC)	18C
Copse LC (FP)(UWC)	20D
Copyhold Junction	15C
Coquelles Control Centre	12D
Coquelles Depot	12D
CORFE CASTLE (Swange Rly)	35E
Corsica Street Ventilation Shaft	49A
Corton Steps LC (UWC)	33A
COSHAM	26C
Cosham Jn	26C
Cosham LC (CCTV)	26C
Cottage Bridge	14C
Cottage Jn	14C
Coulsden North GF	14C
COULSDON SOUTH	14C, 15A
Court Loop Junction South	3B
Courthill Loop Jns	3A, 4
Couston Botton LC (UWC)	33A
COVENT GARDEN	45C
Cow Lane Bridge	3A, 4
Cow Lane LC	20C
Cow LC (UWC)	17A

Holyhead Close Tunnell (DLR)	48
Holywell Viaduct	46B
HONITON	34B
(Honiton Incline Box)	34A
Honiton SB (HN)	34B
Honiton Tunnel	34A
HONOR OAK PARK	4
Hoo Jn	7
HOO JUNCTION STAFF HALT	7
HOOK	24C
Hopes LC (UWC)	9A
Hoplands Farm LC (UWC)	9A, 9B
Hoppity Tunnel	14C
HORLEY	15B
HORNCHURCH	45B
HORSHAM	19B
Horsham Jn	19B
Horsham Road LC (CCTV)	19B
HORSLEY	23
HORSTED KEYNES (Bluebell)	35D
Horton LC (UWC)(NT)	9B
Hothfleld	11A
HOUNSLOW	1L
HOUNSLOW CENTRAL	43D
HOUNSLOW EAST	43D
Hounslow Jn	1L, 25A
HOUNSLOW WEST	43D
HOVE	16
Hove Jn	16
Hove Tunnel	16
Howell's LC (UWC)	30A
HOXTON	46B
Hulbury LC (FP) (UWC)	7
Humbers LC (FP)(UWC)	33C
Hungerford Bridge	3A
Hunter LC (UWC)	35A
Hunts Path LC (FP)(UWC)	33C
Hunts Path No.2 LC (UWC)	33C
Hurdcott Lodge LC (UWC)	33B
HURST GREEN	14B
Hurstborne Viaduct	32A
Hutchings LC	20C
Hyde LC (UWC)	35A
HYDE PARK CORNER	45C
Hyford LC (UWC)	31B
Hythe (Hants)	30A
HYTHE (RHDR)	18E
HYTHE PIER RAILWAY	30A
ICKENHAM	42A
(Idmiston)	32B
Idsworth LC (UWC)	26B
IFIELD	19B
Imberhorne or Hill Place Viaduct	14B
IMPERIAL WHARF	1R, 2L
Inlands Road LC (AHBC)	20D
International Boundary (England/France)	12C
International Jn	2R
Intersection Tunnel	41A
ISFIELD (Lavender Line)	16A
ISLAND GARDENS (DLR)	48
ISLE OF WIGHT STEAM RAILWAY	35C
ISLEWORTH	1L
Itchen River Bridge	29
(Itchingfield Jn)	19C
Itford LC (R/G)	17A
Jackson's LC (FP)(UWC)	30A
Jacob's Gutter Lane LC (AHBC)	30A
Jacobs No.1 LC (UWC)	7
Jenkins Hill LC (UWC)	25B
Jersey Sidings	31D
Jonse's LC (UWC)	35C
JUBILEE LINE	42, 43A
KEARSNEY	13
Kearsney Viaduct	13
(Kemp Town Jn)	16
Kemps Farm LC (UWC)	15C
KEMPTON PARK	21B
KEMSING	7
KEMSLEY	8B
KENLEY	14C
Kennardington LC (AHBC)	18D
Kennet & Avon Canal	27A
KENNINGTON	39B
KENSAL GREEN	41A
Kensal Green Jn (High Level Line)	1R
Kensal Green Tunnel	1R, 41A
KENSINGTON (OLYMPIA) (LUL)	1R
(Kensington Jn)	1R
KENSINGTON OLYMPIA	1R, 44A
Kensington Sidings (Clapham Jn)	1R, 2L
KENT & EAST SUSSEX RAILWAY	13A
KENT HOUSE	4
KENTISH TOWN	39A
KENTON	41A
KEW BRIDGE	1L
Kew Bridge	1L, 44A
Kew East Jn SB (KE)	1L
KEW GARDENS	1L, 44A

Keymer Jn Road LC (CCTV)	15C
Keymer Junction	15C
Keysworth LC (UWC)	31B
KIDBROOKE	5
Kidbrooke Tunnel	5
KILBURN	42B
KILBURN PARK	41B
Kilnwood LC (UWC)	19B
Kimbridge LC (AHBC)	32C
KING GEORGE V (DLR)	48
KING HENRY'S DRIVE (Tramlink)	47C
King Street LC	18D
Kings Court LC (FP)(UWC)	33C
KINGS CROSS ST PANCRAS	39B, 40C, 44B, 45C
KINGS CROSS THAMESLINK	44B
Kings Fernsden LC (AHBC)	26B
KINGSBURY	42A
KINGSCOTE (Bluebell)	35D
Kingsfold Cross LC (UWC)	19A
(Kingsley Road Jn) (LU)	43D
KINGSTON	21B
Kingston Bridge	21B
Kingston Tunnel	16
KINGSWOOD	14C
Kingswood Tunnel	14C
Kingsnorth (former Sidings GF)	7
Knight's Hill Tunnel	4
Knighton No.38A LC (UWC)	31B
KNIGHTSBRIDGE	45C
KNOCKHOLT	6A
Knowle Hill LC (FP)(UWC)	33D
Knowle Viaduct	28B
LADBROOKE GROVE	44A
Lady Howard LC (UWC)	22
LADYWELL	3A, 4
Ladywell Jn	3A, 4
LAKE	35C
Lake Lane LC (UWC)	20C
LAMBETH NORTH	41B
Lambrook LC (FP)(UWC)	35B
(Lampton Jn) (LU)	43D
LANCASTER GATE	37C
LANCING	20A
Lancing LC (CCTV)	20A
Lancing SB (LG)	20A
Landgate Bridge	18D
LANGDON PARK (DLR)	48
(Langford)	33A
Langmeads LC No.1 (UWC)	20B
Laslett LC (UWC)	9A
Latchmere No.1 (Main) Jn	1R, 2L
Latchmere No.2 (SW) Jn	1R, 2L
Latchmere No.3 (Waterloo) Jn	1R, 2L
Latchmere No.3 (Waterloo) Jn	2L
(Lavender Hill Jn)	1R, 2R
LAVENDER LINE	16A
Laverstock North Jn	32B
Laverstock South Jn	32B
LC (UWC)	7
LEATHERHEAD	22
Leatherhead Jn	22
LEBANON ROAD (Tramlink)	47C
LEE	5
Lee Loop Junction	3B, 5
Lee Spur Junction	3B, 5
LEICESTER SQUARE	39B, 45C
LEIGH (Kent)	10B
Leigham Court Tunnel	4
Leigham Junction	4
Leigham Tunnel	4
Leitram No.1 LC	10C
LENHAM	11A
Lenham Crossover	50B
Lenham Heath Loops	50B
Lenthay LC (UWC)	33C
LES FONTINETTES	12D
Lewell LC No.39 (UWC)	31B
LEWES	16
Lewes East Jn	17A
Lewes GF	16
Lewes Jn	16
Lewes SB (LW)	16
Lewes Tunnel	16
LEWISHAM	3A, 4, 5
LEWISHAM (DLR)	48
Lewisham Crossover Junctions	3A, 4
Lewisham Vale Junction	3A, 4
LEYTON	38A
LEYTONSTONE	38A
Lichfield Tunnel	27B
Lillie Bridge Depot (LU)	44A
Limpsfield Tunnel	14B
Linford Street Junction	2R
Lingfield GF	14B
Lingfield Racecourse LC (FP)	14B
Linton Road Viaduct	18C
Liss Common LC (AHBC)	26B
Liss Forest LC (FP)(UWC)	26B
Liss LC (CCTV)	26B
Little Browns Tunnels	10A, 14B

Little Bullsdown LC (UWC)	24B
Little Preston LC (UWC)	7
LITTLEHAVEN	19B
LIVERPOOL STREET	37C, 44B
Liverpool Street Sdgs (LU)	37C
LIMEHOUSE (DLR)	48
LINGFIELD	14B
LLOYD PARK (Tramlink)	47C
LIPHOOK	26B
LISS	26B
LITTLEHAVEN	19B
Littlehampton Jn	19D, 20C
Littlehampton SB (LH)	20C
LITTLEHAMPTON	20C
Lodge Farm LC (FP)	19A
LONDON BLACKFRIARS	3A
LONDON BRIDGE	3A, 39B
LONDON BRIDGE (Jubilee Line)	47A
London Bridge ASC (L)	3A
(London Bridge)	2R
LONDON CANNON STREET	3A
LONDON CHARING CROSS	3A
LONDON CITY AIRPORT (DLR)	48
LONDON FENCHURCH STREET	48
LONDON KENSINGTON OLYMPIA	1R, 44A
LONDON ROAD (Brighton)	16
LONDON ROAD (Guildford)	23
London Road Depot	41B
London Road LC (CCTV) (Sunningdale)	25A
London Road Tunnel	7
London Road Viaduct (Brighton)	16
London Road Viaduct (Guildford)	23
LONDON ST. PANCRAS INTERNATIONAL	49A
LONDON TRANSPORT MUSEUM ('THE DEPOT')	43B
London Tunnel 1 (CTRL)	49A
London Tunnel 2 (CTRL)	49A, 49B
London Tunnel Portals (CTRL)	49B
LONDON VICTORIA	2R
LONDON WATERLOO	2R
Long Salts LC (UWC)	9A
Long Valley Sdg	27B
LONGCROSS	25A
LONGFIELD	7
Longhedge Junctions	2R
Loover Barn LC (UWC)	17A
Lords	43A
Loughborough Jn	3A, 4
LOUGHBOROUGH JUNCTION	3A, 4
LOUGHTON	38A
Lovers Walk	16
Lovers Walk SB (L)	16
Lower Barn No.1 LC (UWC)	17A
Lower Morton LC (UWC)	35C
Lower Pratts LC (UWC)	19C
LOWER SYDENHAM	4
Lower Thorne LC (FP)(UWC)	35B
Lucas Street Tunnels	3A
Ludgate GW Jn	1R, 2L
Ludgershall	32A
(Lullingstone)	6A, 7
Lupin Intersection Bridge	14C
Luton Arch	8A
Lydd Town	18D
Lydd Town LC (TMO)	18D
Lydden Tunnel	13
(Lymington Jn)	30B
LYMINGTON PIER	30B
Lymington Road LC	30B
LYMINGTON TOWN	30B
Lymington Town LC (CCTV)	30B
Lymington Viaduct	30B
Lyminster LC (CCTV)	20B
LYMPSTONE COMMANDO	34B
LYMPSTONE VILLAGE	34B
Lyne Bridge	25A
MAIDA VALE	41B
Maiden LC (Elm Lane)(CCTV)	21B, 22
MAIDEN NEWTON	35A
MAIDSTONE BARRACKS	7
MAIDSTONE EAST	7
Maidstone East SB (ME)	7
MAIDSTONE WEST	7
Maidstone West SB (MS)	7
MAIL RAIL	36A
Mair No.2 LC (UWC)	18C
MALDEN & DISTRICT SOCIETY OF MODEL ENGINEERS	5A
MALDEN MANOR	22
MANOR HOUSE	45C
MANSION HOUSE	44B
Mantles Wood	41C
MARBLE ARCH	37C
Marchwood Military Port	30A
Marchwood SB (MW)	30A
MARDEN	10C
MARGATE	9A
Margate SB (GE)	9A
Maritime Freightliner Terminal	30A
Mark Beech Tunnel	14B
Marlborough Road	43A
Marley Lane LC (CCTV(	18B

ENGINEERS LINE REFERENCES

The location of the start and finish boundary of each ELR is indicated by the page references, usually low mileage first. Where both boundaries appear on the same page, only one reference is given. Where ELR extends over several pages, an intermediate page reference is also given.

AAV	Ascot Jn - Ash Vale Jn	25B, 24C
ACR	Asford 'E' Jn - Canterbury West - Ramsgate	11B, 9A
ACW	Acton Canal Wharf - Willesden	1L
AGE	Swanage (private)	35E
AGW	Angerstein Jn – Angerstein Wharf	5
AHG	Nine Elms Jn - Linford Street Jn	2R
AIW	Alton - Winchester Jn	24D, 27C
AJB	Addlestone Jn - Byfleet Jn	21B
ANL	Acton and Northolt line (via Greenford East)	1L, 37A
APL	Appledore Jn - Lydd Town - Dungeness	18D
ATG	Turnham Green (LU Bdy) - Gunnersbury Jn	1L
ATH	Ashford 'D' Jn - Hastings	11B, 18C
ATL	Peckham Rye - Battersea Park Jn (Atlantic line/South London line)	3A, 2R
AWL	Acton East - Acton Wells Jn	1L
BAE	Basingstoke (Worting Jn) - Exeter St Davids	27B, 34C
BAY	Bricklayers Arms Branch (Closed)	3A
BBD	Bournemouth West Carriage Sidings	31A
BBJ	Balham Jn - Beckenham Jn	4
BBR	Barnham Jn - Bognor Regis	20C
BDH	Brent Curve Jn - Dudding Hill Jn	1R
BEX	St. Johns Jn - Crayford Creek Jn via Bexleyheath	3A, 5
BHL	Berks and Hants line (Southcote Jn - Patney & Westbury Jn)	27A
BJN	Bromley Jn - Norwood Jn	4
BKE	Basingstoke Branch (Reading Westbury line Jn - Basingstoke)	27A, 27B
BLI	Brighton (West Coast) - Littlehampton	16, 20C
BLP	Brockenhurst - Lymington Pier	30B
BME	Buckland Jn - Minster East Jn	9A, 13
BMJ	Blackfriars Jn - Metropolitan Jn	3A
BML	Waterloo (Main lines) - Weymouth (Bournemouth Main line)	2R, 31D
BNG	Bromley North - Grove Park Jn	3B
BOK	Broad Street (Closed) - Old Kew Jn via Hampstead Heath (North London Line)	2:1A, 1L
BPJ	Lovers Walk Depot	16
BRB	Brentford Branch	43B, 3:2A
BSF	Battersea Pier Jn (LCD) - Stewarts Lane - Factory Jn	2R
BSP	Battersea Pier Jn (LBSC) - Stewarts Lane - Longhedge Jn - Pouparts Jn	2R
BTC	Blackheath Jn - Charlton Jn	5
BTE	Barking: Tilbury line Jn East - Barking East Jn	45A
BTH	South Bermondsey Jn - Sutton - Epsom - Horsham Jn	3A, 19B
BTL	Brighton (East Coast) - Lewes Jn	16
BWT	Barking W. Jn - Barking Tilbury line Jn West	45A
CAT	Brixton - Catford - Shortlands Jn (Catford Loop)	3A, 4
CAW	Cricklewood Curve Jn - Acton Wells Jn	1L
CBM	Cannon Street - Borough Market Jn	3A
CCL	Castle Cary and Langport line	35B
CJA	Copyhold Jn - Ardingly	15C
CJL	Clapham Jn (Ludgate Jn) - Latchmere No.2 Jn	1R, 2L
CKL	Longhedge Jn (Calvert Rd Jn) – Latchmere No.1 Jn	1R, 2L
CLA	Chart Leacon, Ashford, Depot	11B
CLJ	Clapham Junction Sidings	2L
CMJ	West Croydon - Mitcham Jn	22
CRA	Crayford Spur 'B' Jn - Crayford Spur 'A' Jn	5
CSM	Chislehurst Jn - St. Mary Cray Jn (Chatham Loops)	5
CSW	Metropolitan Jn - Cannon Street South Jn	3A
CWJ	Camden Jn - Watford Jn (DC Electric lines)	41B, 41A
CYD	Gillingham (Kent) - Chatham Dockyard	8A
DAC	Exeter and Devonport line (via Okehampton)	34C
DSY	Down Sidings Yard, Westbury	33A
ECM	East Coast Main Line, London, Kings Cross - Edinburgh	49A, 2:14A
ECR	Eastleigh East Jn (Chandler's Ford) - Romsey Jn	28A, 32C
EKR	Shepherdswell Jn - Tilmanstone Cly (EKLR)	13
ELL	East London Line (provisional)	46B, 46C
EMT	Exmouth Jn - Exmouth	34B
ETF	Eastleigh West Jn - Fareham East Jn	28A, 26C
EYD	Eastleigh Yards, etc.	28A
FDM	Faversham - Dover (former Hawkesbury St. Jn)	8B, 13
FFH	Folkestone East Jn - Folkestone Harbour	13
FJJ	Farlington Jn - Cosham Jn	26C
FJL	Ford Jn - Littlehampton Jn	20C
FJS	Fawkham Jn - Southfleet Jn	7
FLL	Factory Jn - Longhedge Jn - Lavender Hill Jn - Clapham Jn (Ludgate Jn)	2R, 2L
FSS	Fenchurch Street - Shoeburyness	45A, 2:3B
FTB	Fareham West Jn - Bedenham Sidings	26C
FTL	Farringdon Jn - (Ludgate) Blackfriars	3A
FUR	Worgret Jn - Furzebrook Sidings	31C
GEC	Greenford East Curve	37C
GFB	Gas Factory Jn - Bow Jn	45A, 2:2B
GTW	Guildford North - Wokingham Jn	23, 25B
HAG	Hamworthy Jn - Hamworthy Goods	31B
HAM	Surbiton (Down Hampton Court Line)- Hampton Court	21B
HDR	Hither Green Jn - Dartford - Rochester Bridge Jn	3B, 7
HGG	Hurst Green Jn - East Grinstead	14B, 35D
HGP	Hither Green/Grove Park Sidings	3B
HHH	(Holborn Viaduct) Blackfriars - Herne Hill South Jn	3A, 4
HHT	Herne Hill South Jn - Tulse Hill South Jn	4
HJW	Hounslow Jn - Whitton Jn	25A
HOU	Barnes Jn - Hounslow - Feltham Jn (Hounslow Loop)	1L, 25A
HSE	Hawkesbury Street Jn - Archcliffe Jn	13
HTG	Hoo Jn - Grain	7
IOW	Ryde Pier Head - Shanklin (Isle of Wight)	35C
JAT	Waterloo International	2R
KGC	Kensal Green Jn - Willesden (City lines)	1L
KGW	Kensal Green Jn - Willesden (New) LL Stn	1R
KJE	Keymer Jn - Eastbourne	15C, 17A
KSU	Kent and East Sussex	13A
LAV	Laverstock North Jn - Laverstock South Jn	32B
LBC	London Bridge (Platforms 14-16) – Bricklayers Arms Jn (South London Spur line)	3A
LBW	London Bridge (Platforms 8-13) - Windmill Bridge Jn	3A, 14C
LCH	Lewisham East Jn (Ladywell line) - Hayes	3A, 4
LEC	London, Euston - Crewe	4:1, 1, 4:8A
LEE	Lee Jn - Lee Spur Jn	3B
LEJ	Leatherhead Jn - Effingham Jn	22
LLG	Willesden, West London Jn - Sudbury Jn (Low Level Goods)	1L
LLL	Parks Bridge Jn - Ladywell Jn (Ladywell Loop)	4
LOC	Loughborough Jn - Canterbury Road Jn	4
LTC	Loughborough Jn - Cambria Jn	4
LTH	Leigham Jn - Tulse Hill Jn (Leigham Spur)	4
LTN	London, Liverpool St. - Norwich via Ipswich	48, 2:2B
LUD	Andover - Ludgershall	32A
LVT	Lewisham Vale - Tanners Hill Jn	3A
MCJ	Marylebone - Claydon LNE Jn via Harrow-on-the-Hill	1L
MCL	Kentish Town Jn - Moorgate (Midland City line)	44B
MIS	Millbrook - Southampton Western Docks	29B
MJW	Mitcham Jn - Wimbledon	22
MLN	Paddington - Bristol - Penzance ('Main Line')	1L, 37B
MOD	Dinton East Jn - Chilmark	33B
MPC	Motspur Park - Chessington South	22
MSW	Minster South Jn - Minster West Jn	9A
NAJ	Neasden South Jn - Aynho Jn	1L, 37A, 3:19B
NBB	New Beckenham Jn - Beckenham Jn	4
NCS	Courthill Loop Jn North - Courthill Loop Jn South (Courthill Loop)	3A
NFE	Norwood Jn (Wallington Line Jn) - Epsom Downs	14C, 22
NGL	Hampton Court Jn - Guildford, New Line Jn (New Guildford Line)	21B, 23
NHB	Newhaven Harbour Jn - Newhaven Harbour	17A
NJN	Neasden Curve	1L
NKE	New Kew Jn - Kew East Jn	1L
NKL	North Kent East Jn - Greenwich - Dartford Jn	3A, 5
NMS	New Malden Jn - Shepperton	21B
NSA	Aldershot South Jn - Aldershot North Jn	24C
NTL	Nunhead Jn - Lewisham	3A
NYD	Norwood Yard and Selhurst Workshop Sidings	14C
OJS	Otford Jn - Sevenoaks Jn	6, 7
PAA	Pirbright Jn - Alton	23, 24D
PAS	Portsmouth, Blackfriars Jn - Portsmouth & Southsea Low level	26C
PAT	Purley - Caterham	14C
PBE	Putney Bridge (former LU Bdy) - East Putney Jn	1R
PPH	Preston Park - Hove	16
PPW	Point Pleasant Jn - Wimbledon (LU platforms)	1R, 44A
PSF	Perry Street Fork Jn - Slade Green Jn	5
PWS	Paddock Wood - Strood	7, 10C
QRT	Queen's Park Depot Thorugh Lines	41B
RDG	Waterloo (Windsor lines) - Reading	2R, 27A
RED	Stoats Nest Jn - Redhill - Earlswood Jn (Redhill line)	14C, 15A
RNJ	Reading Spur Jn - Reading New Jn	25B
ROU	Romford - Upminster	45B, 2:5B
RPE	Raynes Park Jn - Epsom Jn	21A, 22
RSJ	Redhill, Guildford Line Jn - Shalford Jn	15A, 24A
RTJ	Redbridge Jn - Salisbury, Tunnel Jn	30A, 32C
RTT	Redhill. Tonbridge Line Jn - Tonbridge West Jn	15A, 10B
RVC	Ravensbourne Chords	4
RWC	Reading West Curve	27A
SAL	Westbury South Jn - Wilton Jn (Salisbury Branch)	32B, 33A
SAR	South Acton Jn - Richmond	1L, 44A
SBJ	Swanley Jn - Ashford 'B' Jn via Maidstone East	7, 11A, 11B
SCC	West London Jn - Latchmere No.3 Jn (Sheepcote Curve)	1R, 2L

SCP	Sydenham Jn - Crystal Palace, Tunnel Jn	4
SCU	South Croydon Jn - Uckfield	14C, 14A
SDP	St. Denys Jn - Portcreek Jn	26C, 29B
SEJ	Sittingbourne, Eastern Jn - Sheerness	8B
SHF	Strawberry Hill Jn - Fulwell Jn	21B
SLC	Stewarts Lane Sidings	2
SLJ	Streatham North Jn (Slow lines) - Streatham South Jn (Slow lines)	4
SMS	Streatham South Jn - Sutton, Wimbledon Line or West Jn (via Wimbledon)	4, 22
SNS	Streatham North Jn (Fast line) - Streatham South Jn (Fast line)	4
SOY	Northam Jn - Southampton Eastern Docks	29B
SPC	St. Pancras - Chesterfield (Midland Main Line)	1R
SSC	Streatham Jn - Streatham Common Jn	4
STS	Southerham Jn - Seaford	17A
SWE	Staines Jn - Windsor & Eton Riverside	25A
SWX	Staines West Jn (oou)	25A
SWY	Stert and Westbury line, Patney and Chirton - Westbury	33A
TAH	Tottenham and Hampstead	45A
TAT	Purley (Chipstead Line) Jn - Tattenham Corner	14C
TBH	Three Bridges Jn - Havant Jn via Horsham	15B, 26C
TLL	Tilbury Loop Line	45A
TLP	Bickley Jn - Petts Wood Jn (Tonbridge Loops)	5
TML	Saltwood Jn/Continental Jn - Eurotunnel boundary (Trans-Manche Link)	12A
TSJ	Twickenham Jn - Shacklegate Jn	1L
TTF	Totton - Fawley	30A

TTH	Tonbridge East Jn - Hastings	10B, 18C
UPG	Upminster - Grays	45B, 2:3A
USY	Up Sidings Yard. Westbury	33A
VIR	Victoria (Eastern) - Ramsgate via Herne Hill	2R, 9A
VTB	Victoria (Central) - Brighton via Streatham Common and Quarry line	1R, 16
VWW	Virginia Water - Weybridge	21B, 25A
WAW	Willesden, Low level Goods Jn - Acton Wells Jn	1L
WCS	Selhurst Jn - Gloucester Road Jn	14C
WES	Westbury Avoiding Line	33A
WEY	Thingley Jn - Dorchester Jn (Weymouth line)	31D, 35B
WJB	Willingden Jn - Bopeep Jn	18C, 17A
WKG	Woking Yards	23
WLL	Clapham Jn, Falcon Jn - Willesden, West London Jn (West London Line)	1R, 4
WMB	Willesden High Level Jn - Mitre Bridge Jn	1R
WMS	Sittingbourne Western Jn - Middle Jn	8B
WPH	Woking Jn - Portsmouth Harbour (Portsmouth Direct line)	23, 26C
WPK	Wimbledon Park and Depot Sidings	21A
WTH	West Norwood Jn - Tulse Hill Jn (West Norwood Spur)	4
WTQ	Weymouth Jn - Weymouth Quay	31D
WYL	Westbury East Loop	33A
WZS	Willesden Traction Maintenance Depot Sdgs	1R
XTD	Charing Cross - Dover (former Archcliffe Jn) via Chelsfield	3A, 13
YJP	Yeovil Pen Mill Jn - Yeovil Jn	33D, 35A

Notes